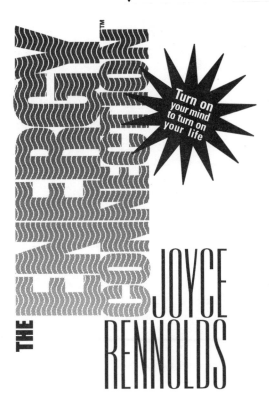

THE ENERGY CONNECTION™

Turn on your mind to turn on your life

JOYCE RENNOLDS

PUBLISHER   *JR Publishing*
P.O. Box 76794
Atlanta, Georgia 30358 | USA
joycerennolds@mindspring.com
www.joycerennolds.com

DESIGN & ILLUSTRATION   *Pamela Joy Trow-Johnson*
artpassions@earthlink.net

The ENERGY CONNECTION™

copyright©1986 Joyce Rennolds

International Standard Book Number 0-9723477-0-4

First Printing 1986
Second Printing 1987
Third Printing 1990
Fourth Printing 2002 [revised edition]

Printed in the United States of America
JR Publishing

http://www.joycejennolds.com
joycerennolds@mindspring.com

*This book is lovingly dedicated to
the healing of the planet through
each individual knowing and using
his or her own "**I AM**" power
to create peace, health, love,
and abundance in all areas of life.*

To Jamie,
May rich and
abundant blessings
be yours.
Love
Joepe Connolds
— 2009 —

Creative Rationale

When Joyce asked me to redesign the fourth edition of her amazing book, **The ENERGY CONNECTION,**™ I was truly excited. Book design is my passion and a creative challenge that, in this case, asks me to visually communicate Joyce's teachings to the reader as if they were immersed in one of her seminars. The task is daunting. Having Joyce as a friend and teacher for many years helped me to build a strong visual concept behind the book.

If I were to explain what **The ENERGY CONNECTION**™ is about in one or two words, I would say energy...spiritual energy. Spiritual energy is about our relationship with God. In developing the underlying metaphors of the concept, I saw spiritual energy as having a verticality to it—as seen in the Chakras and the traditional concept of heaven and *Higher* Power. This is reflected in the graphic devices, such as the wavy energy bars, used to indicate visual "energy" running throughout the book.

Spirals somersault among the pages invoking their place as symbols of infinite energy. Starbursts act as continous support to visualize the essense of this potency.

The human form representative of Creative Substance has been designed so one can personally relate to this energy and to encourage smiles between pages.

It is my intention that my design helps you to absorb these great teachings and support you in making a quick and powerful **ENERGY CONNECTION.**™

Blessings,
Pamela Joy Trow-Johnson
Bend, Oregon

Foreword

I am honored to introduce you to the new revised edition of **The ENERGY CONNECTION™**. Since I first encountered this slim volume in 1987, I have found it to be an excellent resource in my own spiritual journey.

My background is in the law. Legal training requires analytical and critical thinking. For many of us, it is easier to accept those things we can see or touch. Faith requires a willingness to be open to God and God's laws, even when we can't see or touch them. We can't see the law of gravity, yet we all know gravity as a concept exists and we acknowledge its effects. These universal principles work and we can see their results.

Each of us is called to his or her own route to God. For me, as a Christian, these principles connect to biblical scriptures in a way that truly light my path. This book has made me want to know more, study more, read more and open my heart more to my calling. God calls each of us to learn, to grow, to serve others and to reflect the Divine Light every day. God calls us differently, but God never stops calling us.

Whether you have been to seminary or not yet thought about God, the fact that you have found your way to **The ENERGY CONNECTION™** will be the beginning of a process. As you work through these principles as brought to light by Joyce in her own straightforward style, you will be inspired by the anecdotes of others' successes so that you, too, can begin your own journey. Let these ideas open your life to gifts of peace, happiness, joy and prosperity that today are not even in your imagination.

May the reading of this book open your heart to God's abundant blessings.

Happy Travels,
Carol V. Clark
Atlanta, Georgia

Acknowledgment

I am grateful to my students and clients who have taught me so much. I especially want to acknowledge Carol V. Clark, who took the time out of her busy schedule as a successful attorney in Atlanta, Georgia, to inspire and motivate me to revise and update **The ENERGY CONNECTION**™ to be a 21ˢᵗ century publication. Carol could see the possibilities of this little book reaching millions of people to assist them in healing themselves, the planet and prospering. Thank you Carol for your love and support. I would also like to acknowledge Christy Irvine who willingly and with enthusiasm was the person who did the clerical work in getting the manuscript to my printer.

In the *Metaphysical Bible Dictionary* (Unity School of Christianity, Unity, Missouri, compiled and published in 1931 by Charles Fillmore), it is written that by "combining strength and will with the creative processes within each of us, and experiencing the oneness with God, we are able to have dominion over the world."

This personal power comes through wisdom and knowledge as we activate the unconditional love that is inherent in our spiritual nature. The more we love, the more we recognize the presence of the Christ within, and bring this Christ into expression and manifestation.

It is through the teaching of each other that we grow and develop our spiritual potential. It is with profound appreciation that I share with you what I have learned from so many.

In particular, I wish to acknowledge my early teachers and thank the following:

Ernest Holmes

Earl Nightingale

Catherine Ponder

Emmett Fox

Joel Goldsmith

Joseph Murphy

Norman Vincent Peale

Patricia Hayes

The Rosicrucian Order

Charles Fillmore

You can make the **The ENERGY CONNECTION**™:

Let go and let God.

Deepen your awareness of God as Spirit.

Manage your energy to create what you want in all areas of your life.

Manifest your heart's desires in ways that seem like miracles.

*Who are **you?***

That is the question you and God will answer as you grow. This book will offer a framework for you to recognize that you are a co-creator with God. God's gift to us is to offer us an opportunity to fulfill our highest and best good through God's grace. Only you and God can know the plans, the terrific opportunities, the lessons and growth that await you.

Are you ready to make that ENERGY CONNECTION™?

Who am I?

I am known as ***Joyce Rennolds, Motivator of One or a Thousand.***
I work with one person or a thousand or more in an audience.

Now, let me get myself off the hook right away. I can't make you
do anything. What I *can* do is inspire you to look within your own
self to develop a spiritual awareness of your *"I AM"* power, which
allows you to create your heart's desires. I can inspire you to develop
your talents and abilities and to discover your magnificent mind.

It's important for you to know that you are the most important person in
your life. You cannot change anyone else, but you can change yourself.
As you change yourself, your whole world changes around you.

You are the center of your own universe. Your feelings and thoughts
are always creating. It's up to you to put the right thoughts into
your mind. It's up to you to think. It is my desire that as you read
this book, you will become aware of what it is you want, and use
the principles and laws expressed in **The ENERGY CONNECTION™**
to create them.

> *A mind stretched to new ideas will never go back to
> its original form...ever.*

As you read this book, it is my hope that your mind will stretch to
include all the things you want to become, all the things you want to do,
all things you want to have, and all the things you want to experience.

Table of Contents

Part One

UNDERSTANDING ENERGY

*Let go and let **God***

*Let go and let **God***

Perhaps you have heard preachers say, *"Be still and know that I am God,"* *(Psalm 46:10)* and *"Let go and let God."* Some people take these statements literally and think that if they sit still and patiently wait long enough, something magical will happen if they can just persevere and stay the course. There is no question that God sometimes calls upon us to *"Wait for the Lord"* *(Proverbs 20:22),* to teach us a lesson we need to master. Too many people stop with the sitting part and blame God for not changing the situation they are in.

Sitting and waiting are not enough. The Bible tells us that human beings are made in God's image. God is creative; therefore, we are creative.

"Be still and know that I am God," means to be calm and worry-free and to know that you are one with God. God is within you. You can experience God's love when you stop and listen to and reach for God's spirit of wisdom and power within you.

You are made in God's image and you are creative. You have the power to create through the use of your God-given mind and your energy.

What is the creative process? It begins with a thought. We think and choose what we want through our conscious awareness, which is primarily the function of the left side of the brain. Think about this process logically for a moment and how it works in your life.

You remember you need milk. You decide whether to go at that moment and get it, have it delivered, or wait until you pass a grocery store on your way home from work. Your thought leads to a choice—"I'll get it now." You put your shoes on, get into the car and drive to the grocery store, choose among whole milk, 2% or skim milk. You could have easily thought, "I'm not going to drive for milk, I'll wait until tomorrow." This mundane scenario is a simple type of thought.

You think and choose what you want through your conscious awareness, which is primarily the function of the left side of the brain. You map out a plan of action with time deadlines for its attainment. You then get into action doing what you have planned. Then you *let go and let God*. This means you let go of your emotional attachment to having the plan work out just exactly as you have mapped it out.

The right side of the brain is highly developed in creative people and provides valuable insight and power in the goal-achievement process.

Ongoing research into the brain reveals that creativity is not the sole province of the right side of the brain. Thinking and logic functions are not done only in the left side of the brain. Both sides are creative and both are involved in logical processes. The most creative people are those who have developed both sides of the brain. The right and left sides communicate effectively with each other and both are integral to the achievement process.

When both sides of your brain are working effectively with each other and you have released your attachment to having your goal work out just as you have planned, you are able to *"let go and let God."* You are open to letting God provide you with hunches, insights and ideas that may bring you something far greater than you have envisioned. God may have a way to get the job done that is easier than you had planned.

"Let go and let God" means to use your spiritual energy to help you to achieve your goals. By acknowledging the *Universal Laws and Principles,* you are in charge of your energy and your mind. You create your own life.

Who am I?

I represent the Creative Substance from which everything is made.

I can be any size or shape that your inner being wants me to be!

*I am a wonderful **light energy**. I am limitless. You may use as much of me as you want, and you'll never run out of me.*

*I am **divine energy** that is the basis and cause of all things you see around you.*

I last forever, even though some of the things you make with me seem to die. They don't really die; they just change in form and shape. Water can change to vapor and you no longer see it as water. It can change to ice and be very hard. It is still water. It has just changed form.

I must give, for that is my nature.

I am the Living Presence of God that is everywhere all the time.

I am present in each and everyone of you.

I can assume any form or shape, but I am passive. I don't shape myself into things for you without your choice of the form I take. I wait for you to mold me with your pictures, thoughts and feelings. I am pure spirit.

I am a mental conception, not a physical appearance. You must get an idea and picture of me in your mind.

I am a mind essence that is within each and every one of you.

I respond to the faith you have in me and the demands that you make on me.

*I am not affected by hard times. I am enduring,
strong, immovable and steadfast.*

*I do not go up and down in value with
the market reports and I can't be hoarded.*

I do not run out on you when the going gets tough.

I am not intimidated.

I never desert you.

I am with you always.

*I am the living presence of God that underlies
the entire universe.*

I'm here to help you understand how to use your pictures, thoughts and feelings to create what you want easily and quickly.

The ENERGY CONNECTION™

PICTURES + THOUGHTS + FEELINGS= RESULTS

*Everything is **energy** that is
moving all the **time***

*Everything is **energy** that is moving **all** the **time***

The universe is always unfolding, always in a constant state of flux, always spinning and vibrating.

Scientists have explored the universe and all they can find is energy that is moving. Everything vibrates, everything moves. Sound vibrates and moves. Color vibrates and moves. Nothing is stationary. It's all moving, but we just don't see it. The universal laws are like that. They're there, but we don't necessarily see them. Take gravity, for example. We drop an apple and we see it fall. No matter how many apples we drop, each one falls. We see the result of the universal law of gravity, but we don't see gravity. God gave us a mind as the tool to access these invisible universal laws to create our lives just the way we want them to be. Think of your mind as your computer to create and program the most perfect life you can dream.

Three Levels of Energy

There are three levels of energy available to you to be used in creating your world the way you want to be: *physical energy, mental energy* and *spiritual energy.*

1] Physical Energy

Let's look at physical energy first. We live in a physical world. The physical world has an energy that is given off by human bodies. People who have a lot of strong, physical energy generally bump you, poke you, pat you on the back, scurry around and frequently have their hands or feet moving when their bodies must sit still for any length of time.

Our energy levels vary. Some people have an average amount of this physical energy. Others have very low physical energy. They drag around and everything feels like a great effort. Physical energy changes; it may be high one day, low the next day and average on the day after that.

2] Mental Energy

Next, let's think about mental energy. The mental world has an energy that emanates from human minds. This energy is a little stronger than physical energy and is less fragmented. You're usually using this energy when you're at the office, when you're figuring things out at home or at school, thinking with your mind, choosing what you want to be, deciding where you want to go and making that list of goals.

When you work only with mental and physical energy, it feels like hard work, and it often takes a long time to get the job done, to reach that goal and to figure out that elusive solution.

3] Spiritual Energy

There is a third level of energy that operates in and through the universe, and that is spiritual energy.

Spiritual energy is not fragmented. It is a wonderful kind of energy. It is like the lightheaded feeling you get when you're high on life or in love with a very special person. It may be experienced as a powerful flash of light, a strong intuitive direction or a sense of purpose. Its form can appear as bliss, contentment, ecstasy, joy and pure love.

When you are functioning on the level of spiritual energy, you no longer feel separated. You feel an **ENERGY CONNECTION**™ with all. You feel at one with the universe, in harmony with the world.

When you are using this spiritual energy to create what you want, you get things very easily, with little effort on your part and minimal running around in the physical world hunting for what you want. Things fall into place with little or no effort, and it seems that everything is divinely brought to you.

For instance, you may have been wanting a special person in your life. You have thought how this person would be. You've pictured yourself having a good time, already feeling the fun of enjoying your favorite activities with him or her.

Suddenly you find yourself going into a supermarket in which you hardly ever shop. You wonder why you are here. While you are checking out your groceries, you discover someone in line behind you who matches the mental image you have had of the special person in your life. As you talk, you learn that this person loves all the same activities you love and has been imagining a new special person in his or her life, too.

Is this wonderful luck a terrific coincidence? No. It is not sheer luck. It is not coincidence. It is the natural result of the application of a universal law. It is the wonderful use of mental and spiritual energy. People who use these energies know that:

~~~~~~~~~~~~~~~~~~~~~~~~~~~~~~~

80% of their results come from thinking, choosing and effectively using the universal laws to set up the right "causes."

20% of the results come from physically running around to get the job done.

~~~~~~~~~~~~~~~~~~~~~~~~~~~~~~~

This doesn't mean we don't have to work physically. You do. I do. It is necessary. However, by effectively using mental and spiritual energy, you magnetically draw to you what you want. You don't waste time knocking on an excessive number of doors that won't open. There seems to be a current in your life.

You go to just the right store the first time. You go to the car lot that has just the car you want in exactly the color you prefer and it's the first place you have looked.

You want new sheets and pillowcases and would like to get them at a savings. You go to the store that has just the pattern you want and they happen to be on sale.

You think about a friend you haven't seen for a long time and you "bump into" your friend in a few days while you are going about your business. Luck? Coincidence? No.

You are using spiritual energy to lead you to the right place and draw to you the very people, things, conditions or experiences you are seeking.

Energy *is shaped by*

Pictures

Thoughts

Feelings

Desires

Experiences

and *Perceptions*

You form this energy into what you desire through your pictures, thought patterns, feelings and perceptions of your experiences.

You may decide you want to sing in a group. Fearful thoughts fly in: "Will I be able to remember the words?" "Will my voice hold out?" "Will the dues be too much for me to manage?" "Will we be out too many nights with the rehearsals and special performances?"

If you hold on to these thoughts, you will then choose feelings of fear, doubt and worry. You may never get what you want.

Contrast those fearful thoughts with these: "I can't wait to try out for chorus," "I'll bet I will meet some new friends," "Maybe we'll go on tour to an interesting place," "I can't wait to see what pieces we'll practice." You will have feelings of excitement and anticipation.

Your positive feelings about joining a singing group are radiated out and magnetically drawn to other positive feelings about group singing. You may meet someone at the service station and start talking only to learn she belongs to a group that is looking for more singers. Luck? Coincidence? No. Welcome to the ease and speed of Spirit!

Conscious Mind

Your conscious mind is your thinking mind, a precious asset. Bless your conscious mind. It is the part of your mind that sees fingers on your hand and is able to count them.

The conscious mind is like the computer programmer who puts all the facts into the computer and chooses what the computer will work on. Once all the choices are made and the data is collected and put into the computer, the programmer can move on, secure in the knowledge that the computer is going to analyze the data and deliver the requested results.

The role of your conscious mind is to direct the subconscious mind by choosing what you want to be, do and have. The identification of the choice is yours. What do you want? Next it thinks of all the possible ways it can accomplish the task, overcome obstacles, choose a course of action and act on that plan. The conscious mind operates through the five senses: sight, touch, smell, taste and hearing. We're comfortable relying on these five senses, but there is a sixth sense called intuition. This sense is not as comfortable because it is invisible; it is an intangible experiential sense. Intuition is experienced as a hunch, a vision, a feeling, a vague notion. Maybe it's a flash, maybe it sounds like a voice. Learn to trust and follow your intuition. It is a vital part of the creation process.

The conscious mind is your tool to think and choose what you want. Using this tool, you can be, do or have what you choose. Once you have envisioned a plan, you use your conscious mind to repeat the desired result over and over until it sinks into your subconscious mind.

Subconscious Mind

The subconscious mind is the powerhouse that pulls everything together and draws you to the right and perfect people, places, things and experiences. It is a magnetic part of you. Data goes into your subconscious mind and is expressed as your experiences.

The subconscious mind is the storehouse, the warehouse of everything that has ever happened to you. It's all in there. The computers of today are similar to your subconscious mind. What you feed into a computer, you get out of a computer. What you feed into your subconscious mind, you experience in your life.

Our image of ourselves begins long before we can articulate the abstract concept of image. What is the image you have in your mind? How do you see yourself? When you came into the world and your mother held you for the first time, what did she say? Did she say, "Oh, my goodness, we have another mouth to feed?" Did she say, "She's precious?" Did she say, "His father never made anything out of himself so this child is probably going to turn out just like him?" Did she say, "This child is special and will do great things?"

These memories and experiences are stored in your subconscious. There may be memories of pain and pleasure. Painful memories keep causing you trouble and get played over and over like a continuous video replay because the energy from those experiences hasn't been released. Some painful memories that get played over and over are those of unsatisfying relationships. Have you ever had a relationship that wasn't too satisfying? Have you ever ended the relationship and gotten a new mate only to discover that the new one is just like the one before? The name is different but the rest of the story is the same.

Consider a woman who was married and very frustrated because her husband had great ability as an artist. She could not get him to use his abilities. The marriage ended in divorce and the woman married a creative man who had great musical abilities. She worked very hard to get him to do something with himself. Nothing worked. That marriage ended, too. She got hooked up with another creative musician. She couldn't get him to use his abilities on a large scale either.

Finally she got the message. She herself had great talents and abilities she wasn't using on a large scale and even some talents she wasn't using at all. She stopped trying to fix everyone else and concentrated on developing her own abilities.

The point is that the problems are not with the other person. As you hold on to fear, resentment, worry, sadness, disappointment, frustration, guilt, hope and all kinds of emotions from past experiences, you will draw to you more experiences of the same nature. As you hold on to emotions from previous relationships, you will attract people who will treat you the same as before. That is the way the subconscious works.

The subconscious mind is the repository of everything you have experienced. In the next chapter on chakras, you will get a clearer picture of how your subconscious uses your energy to produce results.

The ENERGY CONNECTION™

Chakras

Crown

Brow

Throat

Heart

Solar Plexus

Spleen

Root

Chakras

Energy is a commodity that everyone has and uses to varying degrees. Your energy flows from the crown of your head down to the base of your spine. The energy also flows upward from the base of the spine to the other energy centers of the body.

The body houses seven major chakras: root, spleen, solar plexus, heart, throat, brow and crown. Each plays a fundamental role in maintaining your well-being, balance and creativity.

Root Chakra

When the energy is blocked or stored mainly in the root chakra, a person sometimes feels stuck. He is afraid and feels locked into material existence and the physical world. He finds it hard to prosper because the energy does not rise up and radiate out to connect with energy that is vibrating at a higher frequency. Think of it as a cake of old yeast. It is still yeast, but it cannot chemically react to make the rolls rise. We know we are stuck in the root chakra when we experience feelings of fear, anxiety, abandonment, rejection, loneliness and unworthiness.

Spleen Chakra

The spleen chakra stores energies and emotions of love/hate relationships with mother, father, grandparents, sisters, brothers, clergy, teachers, doctors, nurses and other significant persons.

The image of ourselves as formed in the adolescent and teen years is stored here. We view our relationships from a vantage point of rebellion and conflict. These teen years' images are stored in the body and consciousness but may not have been updated as we mature. These images are like old photographs; they are outdated but still in the book.

For example, you may be a naturally good singer but your choir director, who meant the world to you, told you that you couldn't carry a tune. You then stored a picture of yourself as a person who couldn't sing. The faulty images stored here are not true pictures of who you are and what you can do today.

Solar Plexus Chakra

The solar plexus is your power center. Here hangs the delicate balance of who or what has your power. If you are locked into a faulty belief about life, your self-image, or your self-worth, you feel powerless. You may be stuck and scared to accomplish your goals. You tell yourself you don't know where to start. You feel incompetent, directionless. You believe you can't do the job.

Heart Chakra

In the heart chakra you store feelings and emotions linked to love. Feelings about your first love, husbands, wives, family members, people and pets for whom you feel deep love. The feelings of pain and loss associated with the death of loved ones are locked here.

You store hurt feelings here connected to people whom you love intensely. You store layer after layer of energy here. Sometimes you hurt so badly you close up to protect yourself. The walls of energy build up and you may find it difficult to love again. You harden your heart.

Consider a client who was a young, beautiful woman. As a child, she lived in a family where everyone thought she was wonderful. It was a close-knit, warm, loving family. She married and became a part of a family where there was much criticism. She felt sad and experienced a deep sense of loss for the warm, loving family she had known as a child. The hurt feelings piled up in her heart, and she became more and more stoop shouldered. It was as if she were covering over the heart area to protect herself from being vulnerable.

You hear people say they were "heartbroken" over an experience or a loss. The heart chakra does actually hurt when you have painful feelings stored there.

If you are feeling hurt and are radiating out feelings of loss, sadness, hurt, resentment or loneliness, you will be pushing away anyone trying to love you. *The Law of Repulsion* makes it impossible for your energy to do anything but push away the love you so desperately long for and want. When this center is closed and shut down, the person you really are cannot connect on any meaningful level.

When this center is open, you vibrate and radiate out loving energy. Loving energy attracts more love and more opportunities to love. This positive energy attracts abundance. Blessings in every form are ours.

Throat Chakra

The throat chakra is truly our vocal chords; it is how we express to the outer world our inner ideas. When you hold back your real feelings out of fear of criticism or shyness, the energy backs up and is stored in the throat area. Have you experienced a lump in your throat? That is how the body reflects an emotional response such as fear as you try to share your deep thoughts and feelings. The throat also deals with accepting inwardly what your real wants and desires are. We "swallow" stories, "swallow" our pride or "refuse to swallow" a particular situation.

The throat is a power center for results. When the energy in the throat and the solar plexus chakras are perfectly balanced, we can create our desires by the spoken word. Think of God's power when He said, *"Let there be light,"* and there was light. We are not used to thinking of our throat as the vehicle of the spoken word, and the power of that spoken word.

Thinking about what you want is good, but speaking your affirmations out loud is stronger. Speak statements of your desires out loud, and you literally amplify the power of the throat chakra.

Brow Chakra

The brow chakra is the seat of imagination and judgment. When this area is blocked, very little light or none at all is seen in the inner eye. You have a difficult time visualizing, imaging or creating new ideas. You may find yourself becoming increasingly critical of yourself and others.

When this center is open, your way seems clear. It is easy to see the next step, a novel idea comes effortlessly, a solution to a sticky problem appears from nowhere. When you back your mental pictures with your energy, things seem to fall into place with almost magical ease and speed.

Crown Chakra

The crown of the head is the area connecting to light, energy and power. When this area is open, you feel balanced and in harmony with the world. You are in touch with your inner wisdom, and you make good decisions. It is from this chakra that we glimpse the awesome power of God as the source of light, energy and power. The crown chakra is our link to the infinite mind of God. When this chakra is open, we experience enlightenment.

It is helpful to clear the chakras on a regular basis. To do this, you need to relax your body and quiet your mind.

Bring your attention to your root chakra. See it as a lotus flower opening up. See light filling, clearing and lifting the energy from the root to the spleen chakra.

As the energy lifts, allow yourself to let go of any faulty mental thought forms or patterns. Forgive yourself, and forgive others.

Now see the energy moving upward to the solar plexus, cleansing and clearing out any notion of powerlessness. A good rule of thumb: where your attention goes, your energy flows. Clear out any ideas of not being able to accomplish what you want to do, be or have. Forgive yourself; forgive others. Claim your power. If you have given your power to other people, places or things, take it back now.

Pull your energy up to the heart and let go of past love/hate relationships. Forgive and allow yourself to be forgiven. Let the light comfort you. Feel the presence and power of the light. Feel loved. Feel love for others. Imagine yourself saying to one who has hurt you, "I forgive you, and I forgive myself; I am at peace."

Push the energy up to your throat, speaking out words that have been held back. See yourself speaking out. There may be words of love stuck here that want to be expressed, as well as sounds of frustration. Speak out loud the words you have in your heart.

Now let the energy move upward to the area between the eyebrows. This center is known as the third eye and is the area of inner vision. Let the light move easily and freely through the third eye, releasing judgment and opening to visualize, create and actualize opportunities. Let it then move to the crown of the head and out.

This light may be perceived as white light all the way through the exercise, or you may find the light changing colors and becoming a deep purple or blue as it reaches the crown center.

As you allow the energy to flow freely through you, you will connect thoughts that turn into mental images that produce feelings that manifest into experiences in your life.

The ENERGY CONNECTION™

Part Two

PRINCIPLES
AND LAWS
OF CREATION

Principles and Laws of **Creation**

My purpose in sharing this information with you is to provide you with an easily understood presentation of the principles and laws of creation—your personal relationship with them and practical ways for you to use them in everyday living.

You can have your life be just the way you want it to be by choosing carefully the pictures you see in your mind's eye, the thoughts you put into your mind and the words you choose to speak.

The Holy Spirit

The Holy Spirit

Volumes have been written over many centuries debating the nature of the *Holy Spirit*. As I use it here, I think of the *Holy Spirit* as God's divine spark in me; my own personal way to experience God in me.

In *John (14:17),* Jesus told the disciples that the *Holy Spirit* was with them, but in the new birth, He would be in them. In *Acts (1:8)* it is recorded that *"you shall receive power when the Holy Spirit has come upon you and you shall be witnesses...to the end of the earth."*

In *First Corinthians (3:16),* *"Do you not know that you are God's temple, and God's Spirit dwells in you?"* *First Corinthians (12:7)* says, *"To each is given the Spirit for the common good."* The way to bring this about is to *"Have this mind among yourselves, which you have in Christ Jesus, who, though he was in the form of God, did not count equality with God a thing to be grasped...for God is at work in you, both to will and to work for his good pleasure."* *Philippians (2:5,6,13)*

In *Second Corinthians (3:18)* you read that *"we all, with unveiled face, beholding the glory of the Lord, are being changed into his likeness from one degree of glory to another; for this comes from the Lord who is the spirit."* We can be mirrors that brightly reflect the glory of the Lord. As the spirit of the Lord works within us, we become more and more like Him.

To be able to tap into this power, it's helpful to have a clear understanding of the immutable laws of the physical universe and how to align your energy with these laws to produce the effects you want in all aspects of your mentality, physicality and spirituality.

The Law of
Cause and Effect

The Law of **Cause and Effect**

The law that governs all thought is the *Law of Cause and Effect*. You cannot have a cause without having an effect. Likewise, you cannot have an effect without first having a cause.

You are continually setting up causes and you will always get effects in your life. Think of it as actions and consequences; actions and reactions.

Only you can control your thoughts. You can choose to think positive thoughts or negative thoughts. You can believe good things are going to happen, or you can worry about negative things happening. Research tells us that forty percent of the things we worry about will never happen. They just never happen.

The reason they never happen is because you do not give them enough thought. You don't give them enough conscious attention.

If you were to give them enough thought and put enough energy and feeling behind the thought, you would create the condition in your world.

Thirty percent of what you worry about is just mind chatter going on and on and on and on and on. It's the kind of stuff that clutters your mind and keeps you from thinking and moving freely.

Start quieting your mind by awareness. Be aware that forty percent of the things you worry about never happen. They just don't happen.

Thirty percent of the things you worry about are over and done. These are worries from the past; you must release them by forgiving yourself and all others involved. To forgive means to let go of the feelings and energy connected to the experience.

What is it you give power to in your thoughts? Is there a person, place, thing or experience in your life that is bothering you or has a mental hold on you? Is there an old relationship with unfinished business in your mind? Is there a business mistake you once made that you beat yourself up with when times are rough?

The good you want is right in front of you, but you can't see it because you're holding on to the past. Think of your car windshield in the rain before you turn on the wipers. The image is there of the road ahead, but it is blurry, foggy, hard to see. When you wipe away the past, your horizon clears. You can see the road ahead more sharply. Gone is the fog that distorted the view. Further along in the book you will find techniques to help you let go of old, painful memories that are blocking your good from reaching you.

Worries about your health account for another twelve percent of the things you concern yourself about. The worries you have over your health (or lack of it) can actually create disease in your body.

As you release and rid yourself of these worries, guilt, resentment and frustration, you will actually create better health. Thinking ill of yourself or others creates illness. Thinking well of yourself or others creates wellness. You express wholeness of body and soul.

The secret to aging is that it does not exist. Youthfulness is a state of mind. You do go through a process where chronologically you get a year older according to society, but you can choose not to accept the popular consciousness of the way you are supposed to act and think and do or not do at a certain age. Eliminate the word "aging" from your vocabulary; substitute *"youthing."*

Choose a chronological age when you felt fabulous. Everything fell into place effortlessly. Capture that feeling. Make that your mental age.

*Realize that youth is a state of mind
and the results of how you see yourself
in your mind's eye.*

New Body Every Eleven Months

It is interesting that every cell in your body reproduces itself. The old die away and the new carry on. Every eleven months you get a brand new body.

As your thoughts are of youth, health and beauty, the reproduction of the cells becomes more whole and perfect. After eleven months, you may find that you are absolutely revitalized, renewed and illuminated.

> *Do you want to be healed?*
> *Do you want to let go of the past?*
> *Do you want to get rid of negative thinking?*
> *Do you want to live today?*
> *Do you want newness in your life, more vitality, youth, energy, illumination, enlightenment?*

If so, you have to do some things. You must ask, seek and knock, and the door will be opened. *"Ask, and it will be given you; seek, and you will find; knock, and it will be opened to you. For everyone who asks receives, and he who seeks finds, and to him who knocks it will be opened."* Matthew (7:7,8).

Let's look at how we create what we want, how we go from the invisible to the visible, from the intangible, from our mind's eye to reality.

Think about this statement until you accept it as true: "There is a cause for every effect."

"Cause" starts in the invisible world and becomes visible in the physical world. "Cause" starts in thoughts, ideas, concepts and perceptions such as:

"I'll start a business."
"I'll do good work."
"I am happy."
"I am loved."

Feelings are creative and they go hand in hand with pictures and thoughts to make real what you see in your mind's eye. Think of feelings as the wind that turns the windmill. The windmill is like a thought. It's just a thought until it connects with the energy of the feeling and creates movement. Our feelings, like the wind, turn the thought and set it in motion. Feelings are energy. Energy does the work and turns thoughts into motion.

Where thought goes, energy flows.

You see a picture in your mind's eye. Then you have a thought. Hegel in *Introduction to Logic* reports that you always look toward an object before thinking it, and it is by looking at the object many times in your mind's eye that you then go on to know and understand what you have been seeing.

After seeing and thinking, you develop a feeling in response to the thoughts and pictures. The mind is a repetitive machine and likes to keep doing what it has been doing. Once a thought and feeling get going, the mind loves to keep it going.

As you repeat statements over and over again, they go down into your subconscious. They sit there in the subconscious and take form.

As positive ideas take form in the body, the body begins to express a positive attitude. You can generally see this positive attitude in the way a person walks, in the way she talks, in the energy that comes from her or by the glow on her face. This person seems to be magnetic.

You know these people. You like to be around them. Just being in their presence makes you feel good. Where is it coming from? It is coming from a consciousness that says, "I love myself. I am a beautiful person. I deserve the best in all things. You're a beautiful person. You deserve the best in all things, too."

Throughout the book you will be learning how to use your conscious and subconscious minds to be, do and have all you want. You'll be seeing and understanding **The ENERGY CONNECTION**™ among pictures, thoughts and feelings so that you will be more in control of your energy. Your energy is constantly creating. Is it creating positive or negative results? What do you want?

You can manage your energy to produce the results you want in your life. You are the sum total of the causes you have set in motion in your past. Your future depends on the causes you set in motion from this day forward.

Your future is not controlled by the mistakes you made in the past.

Your future depends un the causes you set in motion today.

Let go of your past. Forgive yourself and others.

Be fully in the present.

Create your future with love for yourself and others.

Today is the first day of the rest of your life.

How do you want the rest of your life to be?

What causes do you want to set into motion?

You have power over this energy.

I SHALL CREATE...

You shape and mold this energy into anything you want. You are free to mold it into abundance and a positive, uplifting, light and free feeling.

That means today really is the first day of the rest of your life. What you think today will be your future. How do you want the rest of your life to be? What causes do you want to set into motion?

Your subconscious mind works spontaneously from knowing the end result you desire and uses information stored in your mind and body. You have power over this energy. You shape and mold this energy into anything you want. You are free to mold it into abundance and a positive, uplifting, light and free feeling. Remember that the divine, creative energy that is the source and cause of all phenomena can assume any shape or form. It is passive. It waits for you to mold it according to your pictures, thoughts and feelings. It waits until you ask, until you seek, until you knock.

Because the power is formless and freely available to be molded, it can also take negative forms. You also have the power to mold this energy into lack and limitation with negative pictures, thoughts and feelings, which produces negative results. If you are not actively creating a positive image or a negative image, you are creating by default. You become a void to be filled by whatever influences cross your path.

In *Matthew (13:12,13)*, Jesus said, *"For to him who has will more be given, and he will have abundance; but from him who has not, even what he has will be taken away. This is why I speak to them in parables, because seeing they do not see, and hearing they do not hear, nor do they understand."* Jesus is saying that he who has shall get more and he who has not shall lose what he has. This is a biblical statement of the *Law of Cause and Effect.*

Picture having lots of friends, money, health or possessions in your mind's eye. Feel the positive vibes of experiencing the warmth of a friend's smile. The results you have been picturing will be manifested to you as you push away negative thoughts and focus on the positive. For "to him who has," (in his mind's eye), "will more be given" (in the physical world) and he shall have more abundance.

If you picture not having enough money to pay the bills in your mind's eye, this cause becomes the effect. Out of the fear of not having enough money, you create extra expenses or get laid off from work.

"Whatever a man sows, that he will also reap." (Galatians 6:7). The picture you see in your mind's eye, the thought you hold in your consciousness, the feeling you have in your heart, all determine the crop you harvest.

You sow abundance,
you reap abundance.

You sow lack and limitation,
you reap lack and limitation.

Pure creative energy doesn't care what you do with it, just as the vacuum cleaner doesn't care whether you sweep the living room or the bedroom. Your car doesn't care whether you drive it to the beach or the grocery store.

Creative energy doesn't care what you create with it. It's up to you to decide how to use this marvelous power.

The Law of
Vision

The Law of **Vision**

Our minds worked in pictures before we developed the ability to think in words. Caveman dwellings have pictures of daily activities of the cavemen painted on the walls. Our mind grasps the picture before it necessarily understands the meaning. We look toward an object before thinking it. By looking at the object many times in our mind's eye, we then get to know and understand what we have been seeing.

Buddha achieved over thirty thousand miracles and many people still follow his teachings today. Buddha believed we must follow eight principles in order to have our lives be fully blessed. The most important principle is "right view." What this means in simple language is that you must get a picture in your mind's eye of what you want. Hold that picture firmly in your mind like a snapshot. To this picture, add the positive feeling of having the pictured result. Feeling fuels the image. Think about the film reel at a movie. A distributor ships the reel, tape or DVD to the cinema but we can't see the movie until the reel or tape or DVD is turned on and begins unwinding. The still picture on the film is literally set in motion. Seeing and feeling what you want is absolutely necessary for producing results.

Many high achievers tell of making tangible pictures of the things they want to achieve. They get their pictures taken in cars they want to own. They have their pictures taken with trophies they will receive in the future. They have artists draw pictures of the office building or home they want to own.

Make a notebook for yourself of pictures that show how you want your life to be. Put travel brochures in it of places you want to go, and be sure your photograph is taped onto the travel brochure so that you are in the picture.

Get pictures of yourself that you like and put them into the notebook. Each time you look at them, think positive thoughts about yourself. Put pictures of you when you weighed your ideal weight if you are trying to reduce your weight. Add pictures of you when you were very happy and healthy if you are trying to improve your health.

A client of mine complained of being overweight. All she thought about was her fat. She talked about how miserable she was, how her clothes didn't fit, how she disliked looking in the mirror.

One day she came up to me complaining. I explained that what she focused on always expands and gets bigger. She could see that she was always focusing on herself, her weight and how bad she felt.

She decided to put the universal laws and principles to work for her. She affirmed that she was "slim, trim, healthy, tight, toned and beautiful." She pasted pictures of a beautiful healthy body on a colorful poster board. She added a picture of her face to the head. Now she could get an idea of what she would look like slender.

Within a few weeks she was walking in a shopping center near her home. She was "killing time" while her car was being serviced. She saw a health club and found herself walking in. Within a few minutes she was signing up for a membership that cost her very little to join.

Within six months, she was the slim, trim, toned, healthy, slender person she wanted to be. It seemed so easy for her. She focused on a healthy body instead of a sick, tired, fat body. The results were astonishing.

The purpose of photographs, brochures and drawings is to focus the picturing power of your mind on the desired result you want to produce.

What pictures are you already seeing in your mind's eye? You can tell by listening to the words you are saying. Your words describe the inner pictures of your mind.

Don't look at situations that upset you and describe them. Don't rehearse them over and over. Don't tell them to your friends. If you are having problems and feel discouraged over the lack of money, don't tell your friends about the mounting bills you have. Ask them to picture you having an abundance of money and paying all your bills on time or even ahead of time. You might say to them, "I need some special support. I'd like you to spend a couple of minutes a day visualizing my having an abundance of money and paying all my bills on time." Don't go into the big story about how many bills there are and how little money there is. Don't talk about how frightened you are that you won't be able to meet your obligations. They don't need to know all the details, and you don't need to spend time thinking about them. Get into the happy feeling that all your bills are paid. What you focus on expands. Focus only on abundance.

If you are trying to heal your body, don't tell your friends how bad you feel. Don't describe every ache and pain to them. Ask them to see you in perfect health. See yourself in perfect, vibrant health.

If you are seeking a new mate, don't speak of how lonely you are and how few good men or women there are out there. See yourself as having fun with the perfect mate for you. Ask your close friends to visualize with you. If your friends are not receptive, release them from this request and ask someone else.

Do not let your friends color your true heart's desire. It is yours and yours alone. Write out in detail the qualities you would like in the person of your future relationship. Then you become that person. Let the *Law of Attraction* work for you to bring you this person. While you are waiting for divine and perfect results, be the best person you can be.

If your car wouldn't start and you absolutely had to move it away from the driveway, you probably couldn't push it by yourself. You could push it if you got enough friends to come push with you. You could not get the car moved if your friends came over and you all sat in the kitchen talking about how awful it is that the car won't start. You could talk for hours about the company that made the car, the mechanics that worked on the car, the gasoline that went into the car and the salesman who sold you the car. None of that would get the car moved.

All of you pushing the car would get it moved. When you enlist your friends to see the picture of what you want in your mind's eye with you, you produce results just as when the car is moved when your friends help you push it.

If you find you are describing negative pictures of losing your health, not having enough money to pay the bills, being afraid you will lose the golf match, fearing you will flunk the test at school or other unwanted situations, consider the power of the written word. Write a statement of denial to erase the negative pictures already stored in your mind.

To deny is to refuse to acknowledge a thing.
To deny is to assert that a supposed
condition is false.

If you have been thinking, "I'm afraid I won't have enough money to pay the bills," write a denial like this. "The thought that I'm afraid I won't have enough money to pay the bills is a lie. There is no lack of money for me. All my bills are paid on time with plenty left over." Visualize the bills paid. Visualize the abundance of money in the world on its way to you. Think from abundance.

When writing a statement of denial, it is important to keep the original wording of the thought while adding to it words that mean to you "not so." Whenever the fear thought pops up, say and/or write the denial statement until the fear thought is erased from your conscious and your subconscious mind. Substitute a positive thought at the end of the denial.

Consider the situation of my client who was having trouble finding a house to buy. Like Goldilocks, this one was too big, that one too small, that one had no yard, another had a yard but no fence. As long as she kept saying "I'm never gonna find a house," she never did. Try writing a denial like my client did. "The thought that I'll never find a house is ridiculous. I will find a beautiful house that is perfectly suited to me and my family. My right and perfect house is coming on the market now." And, yes, she found a great house!

If you want to be a great bowler and have pictures stored in your subconscious of throwing the ball in the gutter and missing all the pins, you must erase those pictures with denial statements and then see yourself hitting all the pins. Write these statements, "It is no longer true that I throw the ball in the gutter. I no longer miss all the pins. My ball always knocks the pins down. I always have a score better than_____." (In the blank space you put the score you would like to bowl.)

Take the time daily to picture the result you want and add feeling to the picture. Look at pictures on paper in front of you and in your mind's eye. Say it the way you see it. Say it with feeling. Keep your eyes on the prize.

In the military, the general has more power than the private. It is the same way in universal law. Some laws have more power than other laws. *The Law of Vision* is more powerful than the *Law of Thought*. By holding fast to the picture of what you want, no matter what is happening or what it appears to be like in the physical world, you can wipe out unwanted situations. When water is boiled, sugar has no choice but to dissolve. Seeing pictures of abundance dissolves conditions of lack and limitation.

Pictures and feelings have more power to create than thoughts do.

WHAT YOU SEE AND FEEL IS TRULY WHAT YOU GET.

When Jesus caused Lazarus to come back to life, his words showed the pictures he was holding fast in his mind. He was seeing life and wholeness. You can't hold on to pictures of disease and get health. You can't hold on to pictures of poverty and get plenty. You can't call yourself a victim and be whole. You must see God's limitless substance being formed into an abundance of money, friends, health, happiness, peace of mind, material possessions and any good thing you want.

Layering statements of positive affirmation on top of imagined pictures of lack and limitation will not produce positive results. What you see can wipe out what you say. Seeing pictures of not enough can cancel out affirmations of plenty. What you see and feel is what you get. Keep your eyes on the goal and see it the way you truly want it to be. Keep your words and feelings lined up with the picture in your mind—your true desire.

You set the Law of Cause and Effect into motion by what you see in your mind's eye, what you think and how you feel.

The ENERGY CONNECTION™

Housewife Becomes International Lecturer

This headline is really the story of my life. Let me tell you my story.

I grew up in the beautiful state of Michigan. My father migrated from Germany and my mother was first-generation Polish. I grew up in an ethnic neighborhood in Detroit, later moving to the suburbs. I married at 19 years of age, not wanting to be an "old maid," which was the tag that you received if you weren't married by the time you were 21 in the 1950's.

As a married woman, raising my children, I listened to *My True Story* on the radio. Immediately following was a five minute radio program narrated by a man named Earl Nightingale. I was so impressed with his message. He actually said the "strangest secret" is that we become what we think about. What a revelation! Here I was with a year-old daughter born with deformities in her hip, legs and feet, washing clothes on Monday and ironing on Tuesday and feeling sorry for myself. Was I truly going to become what I thought about? I decided then and there that I would learn what Mr. Nightingale knew and then I would do what he did. Think for myself and make choices that were right for me. Motivate people into thinking for themselves and making choices that were right for them.

After several years of marriage, I found myself frustrated because I was having difficulty creating the successful life I wanted. I crashed into alcoholism with cirrhosis of the liver. I lay in the intensive care unit of the hospital being told that I was going to die. I remember thinking, "I have nothing to live for." I knew my marriage was over, my two daughters didn't like me very much and I hated myself. I passed through a tunnel and heard a voice that said, "No, not yet my child," and the next thing I knew I was looking at my body from the ceiling. When I came to, I saw a beautiful nurse standing over me who said, "You will live," and I never saw her again. I felt an energy in the hospital room that was sustaining me, holding me, loving me. I recovered even though the doctor told me I would never have any quality of life. I made him a liar. My husband divorced me and my hospitalization insurance got canceled. I could no longer go to the hematologist or other doctors. My spleen was to be removed and I had many medical problems. I had little money so I began to study alternative types of healing. Fast forward to now. Today I am healthy, full of energy and look 20 years younger than my actual age. And I now have a healthy spleen!

I continued to grow and was hired by an organization called *Earl Nightingale Communications* located in Peachtree Center in Atlanta, Georgia, where I learned all the wonderful success principles that Earl Nightingale talks about in his *Lead the Field* series. I later formed my own *Earl Nightingale Communications* company where I sold tapes and began doing lectures on motivation.

My recovery from alcohol and disease was helped by joining a *12-Step Program*. This intentional growth led me to the study of metaphysics and healing. Today I am a non-denominational ordained minister, a parapsychologist, a Reiki Master (healing touch), a Ro-Hun Therapist (emotional release work) and International Speaker and Motivator. I have had the opportunity to speak in Romania, England, Jamaica, Egypt, Mexico and many other countries in the world, as well as companies, corporations, businesses, hospitals and churches in the United States.

I share these things about myself because I believe you have dreams in your heart, goals you want to reach, places you want to go in life, obstacles to overcome. *The Universal Principles* will work for you to accomplish your heart's desires, just as they work for me and others who recognize and apply them.

I have hundreds of clients who have used these laws in classes and individual study to create the lives they want. For example, one of my clients was very unhappy in his job. He was a professional man working for Corporate America. He was convinced that people did not like him. He carried a grudge around with him from early childhood, growing up in a dysfunctional family. His behavior was exactly the same with his peers as it was with his parents. He began writing affirmations and scripting out statements that would build his self-esteem, help him to come from a place of more respect for his peers and to look at people in a different way. He decided that they were not out to get him. He visualized himself smiling, happy and achieving in his job. Today, he is a top executive. He has reached his financial and personal goals through using the power of affirmation, scripting and visualization. He used the principle of cause and effect to see in his mind what he wanted and visualized the end result. He allowed the universal laws to handle the details.

Another client came to consult with me at the age of 16 because "his father made him." The young man had dropped out of school and was convinced that he would not return, no matter what.

In my sessions with him, we explored his likes and dislikes. He loved working on automobiles. He decided to visualize himself as a mechanic working happily on automobiles. This goal was accomplished easily since he was so eager to learn about something he enjoyed so much. He loved Ford Mustangs and would thrill at the possibility of working on them. His deep desire to find out everything about the Mustang automobile, how it was built, what the motor consisted of, how fast it would go, attracted him to his own parts business and today, some ten years later, he is very successful and has a very profitable business. His catalogue is sold all over the world.

A very attractive woman, a client of mine, was selling T-shirts in an attempt to walk away from a previous job where she was the caretaker of a group of people in condominium sales who were very dependent on her in business. My client was so focused on everyone else that she had no sense of her magnificent self.

She began to write daily affirmations that she would be in a business that would give her the freedom to achieve success on her own merits. She denied that she was a "caretaker." She convinced herself that she was the most important person in her life and that the perfect job was waiting for her. She raised her prosperity consciousness, learned everything she could about people, did picture boards where she could focus on success and acted as though she were in the new job and doing very well financially and emotionally.

She was attracted to real estate and now sells two and three-million dollar homes. She is her own boss. She is an excellent, well informed agent, who understands her clients and is sought after by people from all over the world who are looking for beautiful homes to buy.

She came to realize that the T-shirt business, a low paying job, had been the perfect bridge to help her become self-reliant rather than co-dependent. This step of getting into a small business enabled her to see her potential as an independent sales agent, and led her to the amazing success she has had as a heavy-hitter real estate agent.

Energy Is Governed by
Impersonal Laws

Energy is governed by impersonal laws. The laws work for everyone. The laws are working in your life whether you realize it or not. Just as in our justice system, ignorance of the laws will not excuse you from their effect. You are always setting up causes by the pictures you see, the thoughts you think, the feelings you have, what and who you listen to and the choices you make. You are always experiencing the effects of those causes.

You set the causes into motion and mold the energy into whatever you choose. Remember that "I can" assume any form or shape:

Friends

Health

Money

Careers

Peace of mind

Happiness

Doing well in school

Spiritual and material possessions of all kinds

As you go about creating your life just the way you want it to be, one of the things that slows down the result you are creating is doubt.

Doubt is a lack of certainty about the truth or reliability of a situation or person. You may start wondering if all this good stuff is true. You may wonder if the universal laws really do work all the time for all the people. It seems too simple, too easy.

Perhaps you received a ticket for speeding but another time you just got a warning when you were going the same speed both times. Based on that, you may wonder if the universal laws are any more consistent than human laws. The answer is yes, they are completely consistent. They work for everyone, all the time.

Doubt is also a questioning of whether you can meet a given challenge. It's easy to confuse doubt with anxiety or a fear of failure or fear of success. Many times you create fear of success when actually you are just not sure you can do all you will be called upon to do once you get the success you want. You may not do it all perfectly but you will surely be able to do the job. You always have the ability to do anything you have the desire to do.

James Allen in *As A Man Thinketh* states that he who has conquered doubt and fear has conquered failure. Think about that for a minute. He who has conquered doubt and fear has conquered failure. The opposite of doubt is faith. The opposite of fear is confidence. The opposite of failure is success. He who has conquered faith and confidence has conquered success.

So how can we move from doubt to faith when fear pops up in our minds?

Doubt may creep in because your mind understands how to do something but your body hasn't yet had the experience.

You may understand how to swing a tennis racket but you have never hit a good shot and your body doesn't know how it feels to do that.

What's Doubt?

How Do You Get It?

Doubt pops up when you give your conscious mind too many instructions at once and make them too complicated. We go into overload and shut down the positive messages. The mind just receives the information. Which thought should take precedence?

To avoid doubt and increase faith and belief, be here right now, do the very best you can and keep your eyes on the goal. Quiet your mind and focus on the top priority of the moment. You can think about your grocery list later. You can worry about your boss tomorrow. Right now, what is it I want to accomplish? What can I do right now? What choice will I make in this minute?

How To Handle Doubt

1. Make your long range plans and break them down into action steps that are easily accomplished daily. Take one day at a time.

2. Keep the instructions you give yourself super simple. Use the shortest words possible and keep the sentences or phrases as short as you can.

3. Relax and keep your attention in the here and now.

Keep your mind where your body is. Be right here right now. Give your undivided attention to what you are doing. If a thought that you might not be able to get the job done or win the race or lose weight jumps into your mind, realize YOU are the person who made that thought up. Realize you are the person who received that thought from someone else and change the thought. See what you really want. Keep your eyes on the prize. Change the thought.

No one is in your head but you. You are the traffic cop choosing which thoughts to permit to pass through the intersection. When you are right here right now, you see more of what is going on. You hear more of what is being said. You aren't afraid of failing. You are not remembering what you did or didn't do before. "Before" doesn't matter to God. "Before" doesn't matter to universal law. Now is where you are. Live in the moment. Your thoughts, feelings, perceptions and ideas in this moment will create your experiences of the next moment, next hour, next day, next week, next year, even ten and twenty years from now.

The negative past only affects the future if you choose to drag it with you into what you are doing right now.

To avoid doubt and increase faith and belief, be here right now, do the very best you can, and keep your eyes on the goal.

Faith and relaxation go hand in hand with your belief that you can do it. Relaxation is a key ingredient to creating with pure spiritual energy.

Relax your mind by thinking first of something you do. Think of something that's easy for you, something that you always do successfully and beautifully. Feel the feeling of always getting in your tennis groove, of always giving a hug to your child, of always playing with your dog. Connect this warm certainty with what you are wanting to do that is new for you.

For instance, if you are very relaxed at the beach and you want to learn to play tennis really well, you connect the idea of sitting on the beach, in the sand, with waves lapping and playing tennis by thinking thoughts like these:

"Just as easily as I close my eyes and see myself at the beach, I see myself playing tennis really well. The same way I enjoy myself at the beach, I enjoy playing tennis. Just as I see and feel the sun shining on me, I see and feel myself playing tennis really well."

You can use these thoughts to create any result you want, such as, "The same way I enjoy feeling the sun shining on me, I now enjoy closing the sale of this property."

Let's say that you hate oysters. "Just as I don't bother my stomach with oysters, I don't bother my mind with thoughts of not being able to play tennis well." No way would you eat oysters. No way. The point is the food needs to be one for which you have a strong dislike for the statement to have meaning for you. Here are some other examples of connecting thoughts: "With the same enthusiasm that I play on the beach, I practice my piano lessons."

"With the same ease that I brush my teeth, I deposit at least $10,000 in my bank account each and every month."

Remember to think thoughts that relax your mind. Your creative mind works best in relaxation, so keep your mind and body relaxed with thoughts and feelings of things you do easily. Choose activities you thoroughly enjoy. Be sure they are easy and that you are always successful with them.

Connecting thoughts with positive feelings is powerful. Connect these positive feelings to thoughts of new goals you want to achieve. Repeat these statements daily for at least twenty-one days in a row or until you have achieved your goal. It takes consistency for the new thought to become second nature.

Give Up Feelings of Unworthiness

Our feelings of unworthiness block our greater good. When you think of the universal laws and realize that you have the power to create anything you want, set any cause you want to set and thereby get that effect, you glimpse the limitless, divine, creative energy just waiting to be tapped. It never says no to you. It does not refuse to form itself into whatever you have chosen. You have free will. It never says to you, "Oh, I won't let you shape me into that." The sugar in the boiling water never says, "I refuse to dissolve." It is moldable; it follows your command. The universe is always saying, "Yes!"

You are the master of your own ship. You are free to use your creativity to mold creative energy in whatever way you choose.

You have just as much freedom with creative energy as you have with your broom or your hammer.

Does your broom feel unworthy to sweep the living room and insist on only sweeping the carpet inside closets?

Does your hammer feel unworthy to drive large nails into wood and insist on only being used for tacks?

Does your vacuum cleaner feel unworthy to tackle table crumbs?

These metaphors may seem silly to you to think of a hammer or broom or vacuum cleaner objecting to doing certain jobs, but the truth is that the creative energy doesn't have any more control over what is created with it than your broom or hammer or vacuum cleaner has over where it is used.

Feelings of unworthiness are caused by pictures and thoughts in your own mind.

Only you have the power to stop those thoughts and feelings. Decide today to stop. Just say no to negative pictures, thoughts and feelings!

Choose to say yes to positive choices that advance your heart's desires.

Maybe your self-esteem is intact, no issues of unworthiness at all. Maybe your issue is fractured energy–too busy! You are into so many things at once that your energy is scattered in many directions. To produce a result, you must have your energy focused. When your energy is sent in many directions at the same time, it is like a garden hose with lots of leaks. A little water is being dropped on several small spots, but the garden at the end of the hose gets only a dribble.

Eventually the garden dries up and dies just as the excitement you originally had about your goal withers away and dies, and you give up the dream. This doesn't mean you can't do several projects at once and have them all be successful. You can, but you must give your full attention to each project while you are working on it. Don't allow your mind to think about three other tasks while you are working on one. When you prioritize the projects you are working on and focus on one while you are doing it, it is like patching the holes in the hose, so the garden gets a good watering. When your project gets its full share of your creative energy, miracles happen.

The Law of **Radiation** **and Attraction**

The Law of **Radiation and Attraction**

Just as heat radiates out from radiators and electric heaters, energy radiates out from people and things. What you see, think and feel within you is sent out into the world. You draw back to you those thoughts and feelings you have sent out. It is said that birds of a feather flock together. People feel comfortable together because they are radiating (sending out) the same pictures, thoughts and feelings and receiving those thoughts back.

In relationships, you attract people into your life according to your pictures, thoughts and feelings. In jobs, you attract employees, clients or employers to you according to the pictures, thoughts and feelings that are being radiated. If you don't like what's going on for you, or you don't like who you are flocking with, change the pictures, thoughts and feelings you are radiating out.

When results are delayed and you don't get what you want, it is possible that you are seeing negative pictures. These negative pictures produce thoughts of doubt and feelings of scarcity. If you radiate negative out, you attract negative. Negative attracts negative.

If you're seeing the picture but not feeling the feeling, your results may be delayed. Remember the wind that pushes the windmill. Remember the movie does not roll without the switch being turned on to set the reel, DVD or tape in motion. Do whatever you can to get the feeling.

Try on the clothes you want even if you don't have the money yet to purchase them. Get your picture taken in the clothes. Take a test drive in that special car and get the feeling of owning it. Get your picture taken in the car.

Watch videos or movies of people doing fun things together that you want to do with that new "special" person you are attracting into your life. If you are working for an award that includes being driven around in a chauffeured limousine, hire a limousine for an hour to get the feeling of being driven around. Get dressed up just as you would be when you were being honored for the achievement. Have your picture taken.

Get the positive feeling, then radiate out the feeling so it can be received by people who are wanting what you are wanting. Think of your energy being sent out and picked up by people just as radio waves are sent out from the broadcasting station and picked up by radios.

Once you have radiated out the energy, you must bring it back to you. You radiate it out and you magnetize it back. What you radiate out and magnetize back, you get. It's a universal law. Here is a personal example. Many years ago, I was on a Caribbean cruise, speaking for some Diamond Amway Distributors. I began to notice that some of the Diamond distributors wore a lot of diamonds and I thought they looked pretty neat. I had never wanted any diamonds, and guess what? I didn't have any diamonds. Garnets and other gemstones, yes, but a diamond, no. I decided I would love to have a diamond, so I went home from the cruise and cut out a diamond ring from a catalog and pasted it on a large piece of paper. I looked at it for a while and then forgot about it.

Several months later, I was speaking and chatting with an audience when a woman came up to me "out of the blue" and said, "Here, I want you to have this. It's yours if you'll wear it." It was a beautiful diamond ring. The woman continued, "I'm now doing what you're doing and I love it. You've inspired me and I want you to have this ring."

I saw myself in diamonds. I radiated it out to the universe and drew a beautiful ring to me. I did not place limitations on how I was to receive the ring. I didn't radiate out, "I'm going to buy a diamond when I get enough money." I simply saw myself in diamonds and was willing to buy them or receive them as gifts or prizes or whatever way was good for myself and others.

Health Spa Wins Award

A European health spa hired me some years ago to help them become #1 in the nation and win an award. Since they wanted to get new clients into their seven spas, I suggested the management team should sit quietly and visualize the spa full of clients. One person exclaimed, "Joyce, it's a rainy day and nobody wants to come into the spa." But I told her that was not true. "This is a condition you set up in your mind. Picture, affirm and radiate out that the place is full. Manifestations can take as long as a moment, a day, a week, a year or twenty years." In the case of the European health spa, it took them six months to achieve this goal of becoming #1 in the nation.

Get the picture.

Think positive thoughts.

Feel the positive feeling.

Radiate out the energy.

Magnetize the energy back.

I am the divine, creative energy that is the substance of everything everywhere. I can be molded into any shape or form. The choice is yours.

I am within your mind and body.

I can assume any form or shape.

I can be anything you want me to be for you.

Let Your Energy Go

Sometimes you form the energy into what you want, but you don't let the energy go, you don't send it out. When you don't let it leave your body and mind, it can't bring you what you ordered. Think of it this way. You go to a restaurant where a waitperson attends to you. What would you like to order? You must choose. If you kept the choice in your head, you would never be served. You make a mental choice, you send that choice to the chef by way of the waiter. If you never send it, you never get it back. You expect the waiter to return with your order.

Energy is Masculine and Feminine

In past years boys were told to be aggressive and to go after what they wanted. Girls were told to be good and wait for someone to bring them what they wanted. Cultures developed the idea that men were to be aggressive and women were to be passive. Passive men were considered sissies and aggressive women were labeled "out of place and unfeminine."

Energy works in a circuit. It goes out in an aggressive, masculine way and comes back in a receptive, feminine way. To achieve results, it is necessary to send your energy out and let it come back to you. Every person has the ability to use his or her energy in both a masculine and feminine way.

You send out the energy in whatever form you have shaped it as things such as a new house, an antique car, a new sofa, etc. It works for non-material desires also. You send out its energy in whatever form you have shaped it such as love, peace, harmony, or maybe it is sent out as anger, frustration or tension.

You then become receptive, allowing it to come back to you as the perfect house, car, relationship, emotion or whatever you radiated out.

Let's look at an example of this as it happened to a friend who had to go to Virginia on business. While away, she wanted to go to a vacation spot near water to rest and work on some creative ventures.

Her conscious mind sorted through the options:

1. I could go to the beach in Virginia and that is 200 miles away.

2. I could go on to New Jersey and visit my family, and go to my old hometown beach. That is 400 miles away.

3. I could wait and go to New Jersey next month.

After reviewing her options, her thought was, "I really want to go somewhere near water and I want it to be close to my business location."

She forgot about it and went on to Virginia on business. Once she reached her destination, she noticed three motels and felt on an intuitive level that she should go on down the road a short distance further. It was late in the evening and her conscious mind worried a little about driving down a road that held no obvious promise of a great motel near water.

She went on for 13 miles and came upon a motel right on a lake with a view of water and trees that stretched for miles and miles. There was only one room left and it was facing the water—just where she wanted to be. The motel radiated an energy of loving people and offered a quality place for reasonable rates. They were obviously willing to be abundantly blessed by the fact that they were full once she got the last room available.

My friend radiated an energy of desire with a willingness to not have it at all. There was no urgency in her energy. This doesn't mean she didn't want it. She did. She was receptive to having it but not putting pressure on herself to have to produce the result. When you put a lot of pressure on yourself or others, the result you are trying to produce is either delayed or it happens in an upsetting, troublesome way.

By the *Law of Vision,* complete with the *Law of Radiation and Attraction,* my friend and the motel came together. She radiated out the desire and followed the energy waves to the result. This does not mean that you are not to think and plan ahead. This was an example of getting a desire on the spur of the moment while traveling to Virginia on business and not ruling out the possibility of getting the result just because it was not planned out consciously ahead of time.

When you are listing options with your conscious mind, it is crucial that you list the possibility of not getting the result at all. It has to be all right with you not to have it at all. It also has to be all right with you to have the result. Once you have accepted both possibilities, you then choose which one you want. Do you want to get the job and feel good about it, or do you want to not get the job and feel bad about it? Do you want to not get the job and feel good about it? Do you want to get the job and feel bad about it? The choice is yours.

All energy vibrates at different speeds. Think about the colors we
see as the result of light vibrating at different speeds. Think about
the RPM's when you shift gears on a manual transmission. Your
energy vibrates at different speeds also. Sometimes it is vibrating

very fast and is light and airy. In this energy place you can create what you want by just picturing it. This will lead to thoughts and feelings and a release of energy that seems to pave the way before you to make the task easier. This is a higher plane of consciousness.

At other times your energy is vibrating at a very slow speed, and you feel sluggish. Then it seems hard to get anything done. Working too long at detailed work can slow down the speed at which your energy is vibrating, as can overloading your mind with too many things to remember. You can keep your energy charged up by breathing deeply, fully and rhythmically. Breathe in to the count of four, hold the breath to the count of four. Then breathe out to the count of four and hold for another count of four.

Once you have established this pattern of breathing, breathe in warmth, good feelings, light and love. Breathe out and let go of all negative thoughts.

Feel the energy flowing through you and washing away all negativity and tension. Feel all the tension being drawn out of your body. As you are breathing in and out, imagine yourself charged with energy. See it. Feel it. Your hands may tingle. You may see and think more clearly. You may get a sudden idea of how to accomplish something you are working on.

It is helpful to take a break for five or ten minutes every hour. During the break, don't think about your work. Relax your mind and body. Calm your thoughts and feelings. Feel good about yourself and everyone else. When you go back to work, you'll produce much more than if you had stayed at it with no break.

When you understand a little more about universal laws and principles,
you can begin to use spiritual energy and the laws and principles to
create what you want and need.

You can't make this creative process happen. It works as you allow
it to happen. Spiritual energy and the universal laws sometimes
bring you results in a surprising way. You use your conscious mind
to become clear about what you want. You map out a plan to do
what you know how to do to get it. You then allow spiritual energy
to help you. While you are carrying out the plan you have mapped
out, you get a hunch to go to a networking group that is having a
breakfast meeting. You go and find a person who wants your product
and you make a sale. You may not know about the networking
group when you map out your plan. As you are going about doing
what you had planned, you find out about the group. You don't
have facts about the success ratio of the networking group. You
aren't sure what kind of businesses are represented there. You just
have a strong feeling that you should go there.

The feeling or hunch comes from the right side of your brain. This
side functions quite differently from the left side of your brain. The
left side focuses on logical thought or reasoning while the right side
focuses on feeling or intuition. Your left brain would evaluate the
networking group and give you the thought to go to the meeting.
Your right brain would also check out the networking group and
give you a feeling that you should go to the meeting.

But They Have All The Power

As you are going about the plan that you mapped out with your conscious, thinking mind, you may find yourself having thoughts that turn into beliefs once you think them often enough. Let's look at an example of beliefs that give power to others to control your behavior.

"I can't stay on a diet because the people around me are always eating things I shouldn't have and are offering them to me all the time. They don't help me at all."

"I can't exercise daily because there is nobody to go with."

You choose to support yourself positively or negatively by hanging out with people who eat what you eat and exercise daily or people who don't exercise and eat things you want to avoid.

You have willingly given your power to people who may have no idea of your dreams and could care less whether they support you. They are in their own power world, focusing on their needs. You can choose to take your power back!

The Power Is Not Over There

When you see the power outside yourself, you may give up your power to things, as well as people. You see money as having power over you and say, "I can't go on vacation because I don't have the money." If you believe this to be true, you have given money the power to control whether or not you go on vacation. This sets up a negative energy field around money. The amount of money you have then gets smaller and smaller.

When you have a strong desire for a vacation and are open to lots of different ways of getting the vacation, miracles happen. You win a trip. You get a raise at work that you can use for the vacation. You land a bigger account that gives you just the amount you needed for the vacation. A friend calls and invites you to go on an all expense paid trip with him or her.

The money is not the problem. The problem is the fact that you choose to abandon your creative powers by believing there is no way to get the money you want.

As you love money, as you love yourself, as you love all those people who are going the places where you want to go, you will magnetically draw to you what you need to actually take the trip.

The Power Is Within You

You have the power within you to create everything just the way you want it to be.

Jesus Christ revealed the potential power of our words as he cursed the fig tree that bore no fruit. The fig tree withered away, which surprised Peter. Jesus said, *"Truly, I say to you, whoever says to this mountain, 'Be taken up and cast into the sea,' and does not doubt in his heart, but believes that what he says will come to pass, it will be done for him."* (Mark 11:23)

You have the power to work where you want to work, to live where you want to live, to live with whomever you want to live, to have your life be just the way you want it to be.

The Law of
Repulsion

The Law of **Repulsion**

The Law of Repulsion operates in the universe and causes your energy to push away anything that is unlike you.

In the past I worked with a large brokerage company. The owner talked to me about his agents who have the ability to make twice as much money as they currently make. He was puzzled as to why agents would make a lot of money and then stop selling for a period of time. They'd earn a lot one month and then earn next to nothing the following month.

I explained that *the Law of Repulsion* pushes away anything unlike you. If you can't see yourself making twice as much money on an ongoing basis, you will push away opportunities to make that much money. *The Law of Repulsion* pushes away anything that is unlike you, your pictures, your thoughts, your feelings.

When the agents felt they did not deserve the extra money or could not imagine their good luck, the money went away. A man I know set a goal of $40,000 a year and was bringing in $3,300 a month for eight months. For a couple of months, he brought in $4,500 a month. Suddenly he made no sales for 15 days in a row. When he added up his income, he was over the $40,000 mark. His subconscious mind shut down the sales so as not to exceed the limit he had set for himself. Once he realized this, he adjusted his yearly goal and became the top salesman in his company the next month.

Sometimes commission salespeople know on a thinking level that their income potential is unlimited. However on a feeling level, they have given themselves a ceiling, just as if they were on a straight salary. They unconsciously set a ceiling on their income. Then when their sales go over the unconsciously set ceiling, they shut down to bring the income back in line with the ceiling they have accepted.

This can be corrected by wording the income goal in this way: "I am receiving in excess of $40,000 this year, and there is no ceiling on the amount of money I am receiving and using wisely."

How does *the Law of Repulsion* work to push away anything that is unlike itself?

Everything is energy that is vibrating at different speeds or frequencies.

Energy that is vibrating at a different frequency from yours is pushed away by the Law of Repulsion.

Let's say you want a relationship with a man or woman who is happy, laughs a lot, goes dancing and exercises on a regular basis.

△ Let's use this symbol to represent the person with these qualities.

You are rather serious and invest a good bit of time in reading, watching TV, doing crossword puzzles and other activities that are quiet.

☐ Let's use this symbol to represent you and your qualities.

What you see, think and feel now determine the pattern of your energy vibration. If you sit around a lot and want to become more active and want to learn to play tennis, you will draw to you someone like you. You will draw to you someone who sits a lot, wants to become more active and wants to get into a sport. It may not necessarily be tennis.

By understanding *the Law of Radiation and Attraction* more thoroughly, you will see how you will draw people to you who are like you and push people away who are not like you. You will not draw to you a person with traits that you would like to have someday, but a person who reflects who you are right now.

_____ *Like Attracts Like*

Energy of this pattern or frequency △ will be drawn to energy of the same pattern or frequency: △

Energy of this pattern or frequency ☐ will be drawn to energy of the same pattern or frequency: ☐

When you sit a lot and are quite serious ☐ and want a relationship with someone who laughs a lot and is quite active △, your energy system will push away anyone who is vibrating at a different frequency than you.

Think of it this way. Your radio picks up WKYZ when it is set on 99.5 and WKVM when it is set on 106. WKYZ can't come in on 106 and WKVM can't come in on 99.5. They are both broadcasting all the time, but the radio can only pick up a particular station when its frequency matches the broadcasting station's frequency.

Birds of a feather flock together because they can't do anything else but flock together, just as the radio can't do anything but pick up stations that are broadcasting at the same frequency as the radio band.

〜〜〜〜〜〜〜〜〜〜〜〜〜〜〜〜〜〜

Your energy pattern pushes away what is not like you and draws to you what is like you.

〜〜〜〜〜〜〜〜〜〜〜〜〜〜〜〜〜〜

If you want a loving relationship with someone who laughs, dances and exercises, you must be happy and physically active. You don't have to be doing exactly the same physical activities, but you must be a physically active person. Then, when you are out in a crowd, *the Law of Attraction* and *the Law of Repulsion* will work for you and you will meet a person who is happy and physically active.

Don't worry about how you're going to find this person. Don't believe the situation is hopeless because you know everyone in your town and you know there isn't a likely candidate in the whole town.

One of my clients decided she wanted to marry. She visualized herself in a loving relationship. A business acquaintance introduced her to someone who was visiting from the Midwest. They eventually got married. Even though there may not be anyone in your town now, you are not limited to any geographic territory.

In fact, the sooner you can accept the fact that there are no limitations except those you set, the sooner you will begin to manifest results!

In any given crowd of people, there will be many different energy patterns.

You will be magnetically drawn to people whose energy pattern is the same as yours by *the Law of Radiation and Attraction*. You will push away from you anything or anyone whose energy pattern is different from yours by *the Law of Repulsion*.

After a period of time in a crowd, people will have grouped themselves according to their energy patterns.

Energy patterns are a result of your consciousness. Your consciousness is made up of pictures, thoughts and feelings.

With your pictures, thoughts and feelings, you set causes into motion that produce effects: situations, jobs, houses, relationships, possessions, health and so forth. These situations then reinforce the belief systems you hold in your consciousness.

A Consciousness of Abundance

Pictures of abundance stimulate thoughts of abundance. These thoughts stimulate feelings of comfort and relaxation. These in turn produce results of abundance. Several situations of abundance result in a consciousness of abundance. A consciousness of abundance brings about continued and unlimited abundance.

Not everyone has a consciousness of abundance. In a room full of people, there will be many different levels of consciousness:

Abundance

_____

Enough to get by

_____

Lack

_____

Poverty

_____

Hope of abundance some day

_____

You will draw to you people whose consciousness matches yours. LIKE ATTRACTS LIKE.

What you fill your mind with is a magnet to draw energy of a similar vibration. If you have a consciousness of abundance, you will draw to you people with a consciousness of abundance.

You may be thinking, "I can see how like attracts like, but I've always heard that opposites attract. How does that fit together?"

It is true that opposites do attract. However, opposites attract within the framework of like attracts like.

Your energy field can admit only energy vibrations within a certain range of your own vibrations. Energy that is vibrating much differently from yours cannot penetrate your energy, just as radio programs that come in on 106 cannot be picked up on 99.5.

If you have a consciousness of lack, you cannot draw to you people with plenty of love to give or money to spend. You will draw to you people with a lack of what you want.

Let's say you are in sales, want to sell a lot of your product and have thoughts of not having enough money to pay your own bills. You will draw to you people who want to buy your product but who don't have enough money to pay their bills. You want to sell. They want to buy. *(Opposites attract.)*

You don't have enough money. They don't have enough money. *(Like attracts like.)*

Let's look at another example of opposites attracting within a framework of like attracts like.

A car salesperson is working with a customer. The car dealership has new cars and the customer does not have a new car. *"Have"* and *"have not"* are opposites. *Opposites attract.* Those who want to buy are attracted to those who want to sell. The car salesperson is willing to receive money and be satisfied. The customer is willing to receive a car and be satisfied. *Like attracts like.*

You must be what you are looking for. You must feel there is abundance for you. You must feel abundance within you.

You first see pictures of abundance. You then think thoughts of abundance. This leads to feelings of happiness and relaxation. Your energy then vibrates at that frequency of happiness, relaxation and abundance. You then draw to you situations of abundance.

Thoughts held firmly in mind with faith pull energy from feelings of desire and joy and manifest now.

Pictures held firmly in your mind's eye bring results to pass in ways you have not consciously known about.

The ENERGY CONNECTION™

The Law of
Denial

The Law of **Denial**

Years ago many ancient tribes were able to walk on hot coals and not get burned. Today there are many people demonstrating that they are able to walk on hot coals also. They walk on burning coals that are 1200°F and do not get even one blister. They don't buy the belief that you get burned when you walk on hot coals. They don't judge their own experience by other people walking on hot coals and getting burned. People getting burned give the appearance that walking on hot coals must produce blisters, pain and suffering. Fire walkers don't judge by appearances. They deny old beliefs and create their own reality.

They walk on hot coals and don't get burned because they said they would and believed they could. They saw themselves doing this unharmed.

Don't go out and try walking on hot coals without training from people who have done this successfully. This is not something to be done without supervision by people trained to teach you how to do this. But think about the concept. Just as fire walkers deny the burning of their feet, you can deny what you don't want in your life.

Some examples are:

"I deny that I catch colds."
"I deny I am never late."
"I deny there is a lack of money."

Even if you don't have cash in your wallet to pay a bill, affirm, "I have plenty of money. I am not worried about how I am going to meet this responsibility. I always have all the money I need and want on time."

Deny what appears to be that you don't like right now. Say it isn't so. Then go on to see it the way you want it to be. Say it the way you want it. Believe it, get the feeling of having it, and it is yours.

Deny what you don't want.

See what you want.

Say it the way you want it to be and believe it is true.

Get the feeling of having it, and it is yours.

Declare Completion

In addition to denying what appears to be so that you don't want, it is necessary to put a stop order on unwanted conditions by declaring that they are finished.

You stop driving when you get to your destination. You stop mowing the grass when the yard is finished. Likewise you stop thoughts that are no longer useful to you. Thoughts of lack and limitation are not useful to you. Your mind will continue those thoughts until you put a stop to them. It is necessary to declare completion on that thought of lack, that thought of limitation. You are finished and done with those thoughts. Bring your energy up to the throat area and declare with feeling that you are through with not having enough money.

You are absolutely done with being sick. There is just not going to be any more bickering in your marriage.

~~~~~~~~~~~~~~~~~~~~~~

Put a stop order on unwanted conditions by declaring that they are finished!

~~~~~~~~~~~~~~~~~~~~~~

The Law of
Release

The Law of **Release**

Blessing someone means sending love and wanting only good for him or her. Send out a very warm feeling toward the person—positive, actual, tangible energy.

When someone is blessed, it is like a fresh wind that comes in balmy, nice, comfortable and healing. It's an energy more than a word. As the person feels the loving energy, his or her own energy field is changed. Negativity is dissolved.

The heaviness he felt is gone. His energy is vibrating at a higher, lighter speed. In addition to blessing and releasing people, you bless and release possessions. If you've got anything around your house that stimulates you to think negatively, get rid of it. Your subconscious mind hooks into something and can create within you all kinds of negative thinking as a result of your surroundings. Your environment affects you on an unconscious level. You may need to change your environment, release or let go of the emotional energy along with the material possessions.

As you let go of the pictures, thoughts, feelings and possessions, think: "I forgive and I am forgiven totally." Forgiveness breaks the link with the person, place and thing. Forgiveness means to let go of the emotional attachment to the situation or person. It doesn't only mean being sorry about something that you did. It is a letting go of the emotions attached to the situation, person or thing so that you have space to put whatever you want into your life.

If you want a new, wonderful car and your garage is fully occupied by an old car, you don't have room for the new car. You must move the old car out of the garage. It is necessary to let go of the old so you can get the new. Go through your house and garage and give away anything you no longer use or enjoy. You may want to have a garage sale. If you bought something long ago that was expensive and you don't like it now that you have it, give it away. Don't hold on to it because it was expensive. It costs you more each day you keep it. Stop seeing people who don't want to achieve the same things you want to achieve. Give up the old mental images of yourself.

Consider a woman I know who wanted to become a successful real estate saleswoman. She still saw herself as a social worker with a salary even though she had changed to a career that gave her unlimited opportunity to earn money. As a social worker, she spent much time helping people of limited incomes get things they needed very much. As a real estate agent, she was still spending much time with people of limited incomes. She did her best to help them get properties and put much more time than was required into projects that had no hope of working out. Once she realized this consciously, she chose to sell properties to people who had enough income to easily purchase the kind of homes they wanted. This freed her up to sell quickly and easily. She tripled the size of her average sale which allowed her to give freely of her money to support those in need.

Give up the old mental images of yourself. Get comfortable with the new images of yourself. Go to new restaurants to eat, shop in new stores, and hang out where people talk about things that interest you. These activities and others that you will create help you get comfortable with the new image of yourself that goes with the new goals you have chosen for yourself.

The new image may be one of enjoying playing tennis and gardening after years of hard-driving activities in the business world. It may be one of being well known in the business world for high achievement after years of being behind the scenes, helping others achieve success.

~~~~~~~~~~~~~~~~~~~~~~~~~~~~~

The point is that it is necessary to let go of the past in order to do something different in the future.

~~~~~~~~~~~~~~~~~~~~~~~~~~~~~

Release Doesn't Mean Loss

Release means to let go of the emotional attachment and hold you have on someone or something and the hold someone or something has on you. You and others are then free to do what you want to do deep down inside your heart.

The Law of Release doesn't always mean that you lose someone or something when you release the person or situation or thing. When you release, divine right action is then free to work in the relationship, job or situation. Divine justice will sort out the next step. You can love the people all the while you are releasing them to their highest and best good.

If you have a house you are trying to sell, release it. Give up your emotional attachment to the house. As you release the house and let it go to its rightful owner, that person will come along to buy the house and become its new owner.

Real estate agents often ask me to visit homes that they are having difficulty selling. You can usually pick up on the energy when you walk into a house. People who are angry, resentful, bitter or quarrelsome give off a negative energy in their home that only attracts angry, resentful, bitter, quarrelsome people as buyers.

Others may have a particular attachment and are not really willing to let go of the house. Many agents are aware that people have these emotional attachments to their homes and they know that such attachments can actually repel buyers.

I know of one person who refused to release a beautiful, one hundred year old oak tree that graced his backyard. He loved the tree and felt an attachment to the shade in the summer and the beautifully colored leaves in the fall.

Another person refused to let go of the memories of her children growing up in her house. She remembered good times, Christmas holidays, birthday celebrations and the special occasions that meant so much to her. People such as these can't imagine living anywhere else, yet they loudly scream, "Yes, I want to move." Releasing these emotions will open up the energy to allow a buyer to be attracted to the home and make a purchase.

In order to overcome these attachments, I recommend clearing a house whenever possible. You can accomplish this work by playing some wonderful Bach or Beethoven music loudly in the house for several hours. Baroque music will also work. No hard rock, please. That is a lower energy. Symphonic music vibrates at a higher level, and does a great job of changing the vibrations in a house or building.

Plants are also wonderful for clearing. Plants breathe in negativity from the air and exhale positive energy. Place beautiful green foliage around and see and feel what a difference it makes. The energies of hate, anger, physical fighting, illness, despair and others are cleared. The house or building will take on an inviting warmth.

I gave these instructions to one of my clients who is a real estate agent, and he did as I instructed. After clearing the house, which had been on the market for over ten months, a young married couple purchased it. The wife was pregnant with their first child and delighted in what she called "her baby's first home." The husband and wife were eager to move in and start enjoying their new home. The universal law of attraction brought the couple to their ideal home while the buyer got his asking price and the agent was delighted with his commission.

Man Releases Mother-in-Law

A successful businessman who attended one of my seminars approached me, complaining about his mother-in-law. He said that she talked all the time about nothing and it annoyed him greatly. He said he could not get a word in edgewise. Apparently, he liked his father-in-law and could not understand why his father-in-law stayed with this "uncouth, loud, self- centered woman."

The man was obliged to visit his in-laws once a week and resented it immensely. He wanted to please his wife by accommodating her by visiting her parents, yet he said he was getting sick and tired of putting up with his mother-in-law's behavior.

I explained to him that he had given his power to his wife's parents. They were controlling him. His anger and hate were destroying him. The solution was to release all judgement toward the mother-in-law and look inside of himself to see what was in him that mirrored back the same behavior. To his amazement, he could see most of the same traits within himself. He wanted the mother-in-law to acknowledge him, he wanted to talk and share things about himself, he could be loud and uncouth, as well. He found that he was self-centered, and even discovered that he always wanted and needed to be right about everything all the time.

His healing came when he consciously went into meditation, clearly forgiving his mother-in-law, and asked God to remove all of his character defects. He released his mother-in-law and all of the ideas that he had about her. He decided to focus on her good points and to come from a loving place. "After all," he said, "I love my wife and want to stay with her. I am not going to let my mother-in-law come between us. I am willing to forgive myself as well as my mother-in-law and move on with my life." Some years later I met this same man, and he told me he was happy, content and enjoying life. He also told me that after he released his mother-in-law, a healing occurred and now they are the best of friends.

Father Says "I Love You"

One of my clients experienced a healing with her father just before his death by releasing him unto God.

My client grew up in the city of Detroit, where her father had been a factory worker at one of the automobile plants. Her early childhood was one of struggle and fear. Her father was an immigrant from the old country and a very heavy drinker with a bad temper. He frequently got into fights with his drinking buddies. Over the years my client's resentments toward her father grew.

Many years passed, and her father stopped drinking and changed considerably in his behavior. However, my client's memories were still locked into her childhood experiences, and she found that it was very difficult to communicate with her father. She wanted so desperately to know that he loved her, and yet he never expressed that love to her in words or physical touch. She confided in me that her father would often shake her hand and say, "Best regards." At the time, she could not see this as a loving gesture.

After some time, the father became very ill and was dying. My client told me that she awoke in the early morning with thoughts of her father and how much she loved and truly appreciated him. She found herself picking up a tablet and she began to write a forgiveness list. She wrote about all of the resentments and the hate that she had previously had for her dad. She wrote also about the negative feelings that she had harbored.

As she did this, she became aware of her love and appreciation for her dad. She forgave herself and she forgave him. She put the sheets from the tablet in the fireplace and burned them. A great peace and calm came over her.

Two weeks later, her father called her. This was the first time that he had ever telephoned her. He told her that he appreciated her as his daughter. He stated that he felt that he did the best he knew how in raising her and he said to her, "I love you." The next day he died. My client felt a deep loss for her father. Today she spends time remembering her dad's wonderful qualities, rather then dwelling on any negativity or lack. A true healing has taken place.

These laws and principles are immutable. They don't change. They don't work one day but not the next. They always work. You can count on universal law.

Group Energy Is Powerful Healing Energy

In the process of letting go of old experiences and energies, you may find your way to workshops, study groups, churches and self-help groups where the energy is such that healing takes place. Just as it is easier to push a car with ten people helping than with just one, it is easier to raise our vibrations and dissolve old energies in a group than by ourselves. You give off your energy, which is received by someone else. They get it, build on it and give it off. It is then received by someone else who builds on it and gives it off. As the energy gets passed back and forth, it is increased in vibrational speed and the mood of the whole group is lifted.

In addition to being in a group, you may want to get someone to work with you individually. People who are powerful at sending love energy from the chakras can direct this energy to you. It penetrates your energy field and dissolves any negative or limiting energy. It then raises your vibrational frequency so that you are able to create what you want easily and rapidly.

Woman Cuts Husband Loose

A woman in my seminar had been married for 35 years when her husband left her. She could not release him and let him go. He was off somewhere doing his own thing and living his own life. Still she couldn't let go of him. She had written the statement, "I release and let go. I give up my attachment to my husband." She had gone through the motions. However, she hadn't given up **The ENERGY CONNECTION™** to him.

The woman was a seamstress and finally got free of the relationship by visualizing a pair of scissors and cutting the cords of feeling that bound her to her former husband. She understood finally that she had to stop feeling resentful, sad, lonely, bitter and angry. She had to dissolve those old feelings in order to be free of the past.

By letting go of the feelings, she created a vacuum into which she could fit a new relationship.

Another woman in my seminar was in her sixties and had been married for 30 years. She kept coming to classes and one day opened up by saying, "You know, my husband is divorcing me and I'm not going to give him a divorce. I'm fighting it. I'm here to find out how I can change him." I explained to her that she could not change him. I made it clear to her the only person she could change was herself.

The woman kept coming to classes. Once again she opened up with, "I have lived in prosperity all my life. I drive a Mercedes. I have a huge, magnificent home. I'm not going to go without an income at my age. There is nothing out there for me to do. I like what I'm doing. I like being married. I'm not going to give him a divorce!" Talk about determination! I gently urged her to "love, bless and release him. At least do that." She staunchly replied, "I can't. I won't."

She'd show up at the next seminar and I would think, "There she is again. I'll just have to send her love and blessings." Eventually she came once again to another seminar and this time came running in to hug me. By this time we were old buddies and great huggers. "Joyce, I did it. I did it. I released him. I want you to meet my husband. I've been telling him about you," she bubbled.

You may be wondering how she got another husband so fast. She didn't. This was the man she'd been married to for thirty years. When she finally released him, he came back to her! The freedom to go brings along with it the freedom to stay.

The Bad News

The bad news is that affirmations alone are not enough to produce successful results when your energy is colored by stored negative experiences or faulty beliefs.

Affirmations coupled with visualizations are not enough if they are focused only on the result that you are trying to produce. Holding on to old energy from previous experiences blocks whatever you are trying to produce. If your business is not thriving, if you are not getting sales appointments, if you are not achieving the positive results from any activity you are doing, it is time to stop for a few minutes. Stop phoning, stop trying to convince your children to clean up their rooms, stop trying to figure out how to balance the books, stop whatever the activity is for a few minutes. List the people, things, events and conditions you are feeling negative about on paper. Picture yourself letting go of these negative feelings. This is what is meant by "forgiveness." Forgiveness is the letting go of negative feelings about yourself and others. After you have let go of these feelings against yourself and others, go back to the activity and you will experience the results you want.

The Good News

The good news is that this stored energy from old experiences can be released. As the stored negative energy is released, you are free to radiate out love, which is an attracting energy. This makes it possible to say what you want and to get it right away.

The Law of the *Vacuum*

The Law of **the Vacuum**

This law is simply the idea that there is no empty space in nature. Nature abhors a vacuum. When you take something away, something else is always going to fill that space. People clean out their closets, drawers, garages and attics. They wait for great new friends, clothes, jobs, money and health to come to them. They wait and wait and wait. They don't get what they want and wonder why. Just giving away the clothes and furniture or getting a divorce doesn't do it.

Feelings are stored in your body and mind just as possessions are stored in your house and garage.

Throughout your lifetime, many of you are encouraged not to experience your feelings. As children you are told to stop crying. Boys are encouraged to not even start crying by being told, "That's for sissies. Big boys don't cry."

There are times when people think the pain of their feelings is so great they don't dare feel the intensity. They don't know what would happen if they did, but their belief is that it would be disastrous. They stuff their feelings and don't feel them. Families also teach each other what feelings to feel. In some families everyone feels sad, no matter what happens. The same situations could happen to the family next door and they would feel angry, while the family across the street would feel scared.

Example: The family car gets hit. Family A feels sad. They really loved the car. They are sad that they'll be without it while it is being repaired. Family B is angry. They fuss and fume about what they'd like to do to the person who hit the car. Family C is scared. They are afraid to go out on the road again for fear they will get hit even worse than they did this time.

Many times people think they are feeling their feelings while in reality they are only thinking their feelings. They know they are mad. They talk about being mad. They think they are mad, but they really don't know how it feels to be mad.

~~~~~~~~~~~~~~~~~

The experience of the emotion is still stored in the cells and tissues of the body. The energy is still stored in the energy centers of the body.

~~~~~~~~~~~~~~~~~~~~~~~~~~~

Let Go of Old Energy as Well as Possessions

If you are feeling angry about something someone did to you, and you don't let go of the angry energy, you will draw to you more people who will do the very same thing to you.

Feeling energy comes from thoughts. Thoughts are the result of pictures seen in the mind's eye. Pictures, thoughts and feelings produce results. Any energy that is held onto is going to draw to you more of the same experience.

You may be wondering how you let go of feelings that are connected to people and experiences. When I get anxious, I ask myself, "Who's bothering me?" not, "What's bothering me?" I specifically ask "Who is bothering me?" I get physically still, quiet my conscious mind and allow my intuition to give me the name of the person. Sometimes I get a feeling about who the person is and sometimes it is a visual image in my mind's eye. I realize who it is. I then love and bless and release that person.

You don't want any person, place or thing in your life to have a mental hold on you. Sometimes places and things have mental holds on you, just as people do. You have held on emotionally to things and places.

Love
_____

Let go
_____

Bless and release

The Law of *Love*

The Law of **Love**

Once you let go of things, places, people and energy that were unpleasant for you, you have space for something new in your life. It's now possible for you to radiate out unconditional love for yourself and others from your heart chakra.

This unconditional love energy heals. It lifts people's spirits. It transmutes negative energy into positive energy. The vibration of unconditional love transforms audiences or groups that have been disagreeing and having trouble getting a task done into a cohesive group that gets the job done with ease.

You are always evolving. Energy is always spiraling upward, vibrating at the speed of divine energy. The vibration of the energy is experienced through each chakra.

It's almost impossible to define love because you are describing an energy, not just an abstract thought. You must have the feeling from the heart chakra. When you are experiencing this feeling or are in this energy, you don't judge, attack, criticize or condemn. You turn fear into faith. You trust the universe to support you in the results you are seeking. You align yourself with beauty, grace, harmony, peace, joy and serenity.

You give freely of your time and money and this puts you in a position to receive. You don't give so that you will get. You don't buy insurance with your tithes. You give from unconditional love and gratitude and the windows of heaven open up and pour out blessings so vast you don't have room enough to receive them. Then you have to make more room!

~~~~~~~~~~~~~~~~~~~~~~~~~~~~~~

You reach the state of totally loving yourself and others and know deep within your being that you can have whatever you want. You accept the idea that you can be whatever you want to be. You become the spiritual alchemist and create instantly.

~~~~~~~~~~~~~~~~~~~~~~~~~~~~~~

You love your way totally through life getting just the parking space you want, going through the market line quickly, lifting the spirits of frustrated people you meet as you go about your day.

~~~~~~~~~~~~~~~~~~~~~~~~~~~~~~~~

With the Law of Love, there is no disease, no sickness, no trouble. It is the vibration that Jesus operated out of that produced mystical, miraculous manifestations. We all have the potential to produce miracles by radiating out unconditional love from our heart chakra.

~~~~~~~~~~~~~~~~~~~~~~~~~~~~~~~~

The Law of Love is the Grace of God operating in and through your life. This love manifests as the accident that almost happened and didn't…the sale that magically appears…the relationship that gets restored.

Board Meeting
Productivity Increased

One of my clients is a businessman who frequently attends board meetings. One day he walked into a meeting where the energy was quite negative. The discussion was heated and things were not going as the man wished them to go. He kept silent, radiating out unconditional love from the heart chakra while keeping in mind the results he wanted. His presence was felt and the vibrations were changed in the room. He never spoke out loud but continued to radiate out loving energy from the heart chakra while visualizing the results he wanted. The agenda was handled speedily, and the results were exactly as he wanted them to be.

Love Is a Magnetic Energy That Draws To You What You Think About

Since energy works in a circuit, what you put out comes back to you multiplied. When you put out love coupled with the desire to have everyone you meet be blessed, everyone you meet wants you to be blessed. As you radiate out love for yourself and others, you will find yourself receiving all kinds of treats, presents, hugs, kisses, fun, job opportunities or whatever your heart desires.

Love is the strongest creative power there is.

Love has the power to dissolve anything that is not love.

Love dissolves fear, jealousy, anger, resentment, feelings of loss, hopelessness, helplessness and anything else that is not love.

Create, Don't Compete

You are not here to compete with each other. You are here to create what you need and want with love. As you are creating what you need and want, others follow your example and create for themselves, too. As people are happy and grateful, they are feeling only love.

Meditation

Meditation is the practice of focusing your attention on one particular thing and allowing all your energy to be directed to one thought or target.

The following thoughts are offered to guide you in focusing your attention on clearing and cleansing your energy field and manifesting whatever your heart desires.

The Kingdom is Within

Know that the Kingdom of God, the power of God is truly within you. Get quiet and still. Put your feet on the floor and relax. Breathe in warmth, good feelings, light and love and let yourself go.

Close your eyes to keep out the activity and distraction of the outside world. Breathe in warmth, good feelings, light and love. Exhale all tension from the body and let go. Take as much time to relax as necessary. Some days you will go to a relaxed place more quickly than other days.

Get a sense of a very soft gentle spring rain falling on you. Use your senses to feel the gentle droplets of rain on your head and body. As it falls on you, it cleanses you. As it gently falls over you, you allow it to take all of your resentments, hurts, guilt and shame away. The soft, gentle rain is purifying you, cleansing you, washing you. Feel the rain ever so gently cleansing you at a feeling level.

The rain is washing over you. Very softly and gently the rain falls upon you and, as it does, you feel cleansed, renewed and restored. Get in touch with the presence and power of God within.

The sun comes out and you feel the sunlight on your body, warm and comforting. The sunlight is very bright. It feels magnificent, beautiful and warm. You get a sense of peace. You get a sense of oneness with God and you are aware that the kingdom, the point of power, is within.

Spend a few moments enjoying the experience. Create within your mind and heart the feelings, pictures and thoughts of those things that you want to manifest as your heart's desires. See the pictures, let yourself imagine the feelings as if you were having the actual experiences, relish the feelings, delight in the pictures. Accept the abundance and prosperity you desire in your heart, mind and spirit and know that it is yours. Release this meditation into the universe and give thanks to God for the many blessings that are yours.

The Law of
Giving
and Receiving

The Law of **Giving and Receiving**

As you work with *the Law of Giving and Receiving,* you see that giving and receiving are really two sides of the same coin. It is necessary to give so that you may receive. It is necessary to receive so that you have more to give.

If you are in business and pass on your merchandise to people who do not pay you, you are soon out of business. If you give your money to a worthy cause and do not receive money from some source, you soon have no more money to give to the cause.

If you continually receive from folks and don't give, you become known as a "taker." Many folks will avoid you because they feel used.

When you truly give from the heart chakra with unconditional love, no strings attached, there is no shortage of receiving. You are giving unselfishly. You are giving joyfully. You are giving because you genuinely love the people or the cause to which you are giving. When you give from this space, you can't help but receive in abundance. One of the problems with giving is that people think they must get back from the person to whom they gave everything.

In a relationship one person thinks, "I scratched your back. Now it is time for you to scratch my back. You owe me one." If you make an agreement that you will each scratch backs for thirty minutes, that is different from believing that you owe me because I did it for you. When you make an investment of your time, money, friendship, talent or other energy, the return of the investment seldom comes from the place where you made the investment. Rarely do you reap only from where you have sown.

Think about the way a bird scatters seeds. The wind blows an acorn and a new oak tree sprouts a long way from its parent. An exciting benefit of this thinking is that you never know when or how the benefit is coming. Every day can be full of wonderful surprises.

A major obstacle to receiving your heart's true desire is control. You tell God what you want and then tell Him or Her exactly how and who is to give it to you. Then you try to force the result in the way you have pre-determined. This is a sure way to block your good by insisting that you control the source and the method. The other block to receiving is telling God what you want and then doubting you will ever get it because you can't imagine where in the world it would ever come from.

Let's look at giving and receiving in terms of money. The Scriptures don't condemn wealth, only the wrong use of wealth. Nicodemus and Joseph were both rich followers of Jesus. Money is good and the Bible says, *"Beloved, I pray that you may prosper" (3 John 1:2).*

However, if your focus is on accumulating material wealth rather than on the service you are providing, you are thinking of all the money you are getting. You are thinking of how much money you will have in the bank. You are doing what you're doing for the sake of the money. Please understand that it is necessary to set monetary goals. You need to choose how much money you want to have. You need to know where your bank account stands at all times. You must know what is going on in order to manage your money wisely and to be a good steward.

Setting a monetary goal and knowing what is going on is different from doing what you're doing solely for the sake of money. When your focus in on accumulating money rather than on the service you are providing through your job and business, you have a fear of losing money and that makes it hard to accumulate money. You may get some saved up and then added expenses come along and take it away. You may get new contracts and be excited about the increased income and then lose some old contracts. This puts you back where you were before you got the new contracts. Your friends may see you as a person who really wants a lot of money and the things money can buy. What they see as desire is built on a foundation of being afraid you will lose what you have. For example, consider the fear that you will lose your friends so you'd better have money to buy the help that your friends would have given you. The fear that you will lose your health generates a need to have money to buy the needed medical help to regain your health.

The thought of loss lodged deep within your subconscious mind brings on more loss. Often people who have received a lot of money have given a lot of service. They have focused their attention on the service they are providing to others. They love themselves as much as they love others. They are willing to receive abundantly and feel deserving of receiving all the good things of this world: love, friendship, health, money, material possessions, recognition and prosperity in all areas of life.

As you give a product in genuine love and service to human kind, you receive in abundance. As you give your time and love to a worthy cause, you receive in abundance. You cannot out-give the universe.

However, if you give much service and receive a great deal of money, the money is no good to you unless you have the understanding to use it for the good of yourself and others. You must grow with your possessions until you get the ability to handle them. Supply unfolds as fast as you need it or as fast as you can handle it.

This means your desire for money must be matched with your ability to handle money. Is your checking account balanced? Do you realize the value of money? Do you use money for wise purchases? Do you know how to maintain a steady flow of cash for your business? Can you manage the cash flow so there is money to pay the employees on time? Is your money working for you or are you working for it?

You cannot use money selfishly and expect it to grow. Using money only for yourself is a form of hoarding and anything that is hoarded spoils eventually. Find a place where you feel good about giving and give your money, time and talent. Then expect a return on your investment. The focus is on giving, not getting. However, you must be willing to receive a return on your investment. This is totally different from giving to get.

If you are not giving any of your time, money or talent to others, you are coming from fear of not having enough for yourself and others, too. It's either you or them. From this day on, erase all fear from your mind that there is not enough for you and everyone else. Jesus needed no rainy day fund. The universe was at His command. The mind substance out of which money is created is a living magnet. When you depend on mind substance for supply of all kinds, you never lack for any good thing.

Money is a symbol of God's abundant inexhaustible substance. Substance can't be hoarded and it is always accessible to you. Money was invented for convenience in exchanging goods and services. Bless it, bless others who have more than you, bless others who have less than you, bless everyone and everything and the blessings will return to you. Love sent returns in love.

If you are giving a service and not receiving as much money as you'd like for what you do, you are dealing with a poverty consciousness. Your mind has a fear of not enough to begin with. By concentrating your thoughts on "not enough" over and over, your mind accepts "not enough" as the truth. Your mind believes there is not enough out there for you.

If you inwardly rebel over the way things are and feel victimized, you shut down the ways in which you could receive more for what you do. If you believe there isn't enough and have a fear of lack, you draw to you what you fear. *The Law of Repulsion* will also push away abundance because that is the way energy works.

Ernest Holmes, in the *Science of Mind Textbook,* says, "God withholds nothing by choice, only by law." The good news is that no matter how long you have been holding onto the fear of lack or not enough for you, all the service you have provided to others is on the books of the universal recordkeeping system. Nothing is ever lost in spirit. You will collect the benefit of every service that you have given and for which you have not been paid when you free your mind from the poverty complex.

~~~~~~~~~~~~~~~~~~~~~~

All the good that you have been unwilling to receive in the past is yours. It is just waiting for you to be willing to receive it now. Choose to accept it. Make a conscious choice to give and receive, bless and be blessed.

~~~~~~~~~~~~~~~~~~~~~~

Don't worry about the source. Once you are willing to receive, you will attract to you the ideas to bring to you what is rightfully yours. You may have to provide yet another service to receive the blessing, but the return on your investment will be abundant.

As you are handling your money, see yourself as a steward of God handing out His inexhaustible supplies in the form of money. When you are giving money, don't give with the feeling of giving charity. If you give out of a feeling of giving charity, you will end up needing charity from others. Don't criticize or waste time complaining about "those people" who got their money unscrupulously or "those people" who don't work hard enough or "those people" who won the lottery. That is not your business. Your mission is to give from the heart chakra. That will result in what is rightfully yours coming to you.

Don't give to be appreciated. The receiver of the gift will resent the strings of "needing to be grateful" attached to the gift and probably won't be grateful. Don't give because you think you should or you have to because it is birthday time. It is better to make a handmade card from your heart than to give an expensive gift resentfully.

Don't give with your energy in the lower chakras. Raise your energy up to the heart chakra and give with unconditional love. If your energy is stuck, read, study, pray, meditate, get help until your energy is flowing freely.

152

THE KINGDOM
OF GOD IS
WITHIN YOU

Part Three

KNOW THAT THE KINGDOM OF GOD IS WITHIN YOU

The ENERGY CONNECTION™

The ENERGY CONNECTION™

Let's take a look at the overall picture of the **ENERGY CONNECTION™**.

Before you can manage your energy to create something, you must know what it is you want. A help in realizing your heart's desire is to look through magazines, stroll through shopping malls, read, look at travel brochures, explore educational programs on TV, volunteer. As you look at pictures, you may get a realization of things you want to do, be or have. At times words alone are not enough to give you the emotional reaction and the internal knowing that you want to be, do or have a certain thing. A picture really is worth a thousand words. Pictures help you to know what it is you want to be, do or have when you are in the choosing stage.

Pictures are also powerful aids in helping you stay focused while you are waiting for the result.

Once you have chosen your goal and set your cause in motion, direct your subconscious mind to think positively about the chosen goal. Have faith that you will experience that choice. Radiate out thoughts, feelings and pictures of that desired result.

Feel comfortable in the knowledge that *the Law of Repulsion* will push away energy unlike your energy while *the Law of Attraction* will pull to you the energy you are radiating. Visualize these thoughts like beams of light sending out your heart's desire to the universe.

The Law of Radiation and Attraction is drawing energy like yours to you and *the Law of Repulsion* is pushing away energy that is unlike you. Know that the power to be, do and have what you want lies within you. The Kingdom of God is within. As it is within, so it is without. The creative power within you, God's spirit within you, will radiate out in whatever form you choose and come back to you fully clothed. As you are radiating out the energy of what you want, create vacuums. Clean out your thoughts. Clean out your feelings. Do this on a daily basis. When it is appropriate, clean out your closets and drawers, attics and garages. Give up those old images of you that no longer fit, those images that were never true in the first place. Make room for what you want by loving, blessing and releasing people, things, situations, experiences on a daily basis. Take each day one day at a time. Create each day anew just the way you want it to be. Leave the past behind. Close the door on the way it was and focus on the way you are creating it now. Today God gives us a new choice. Make good choices.

Take time to lift your energy through meditation or prayer. Meditation does not have to be a lengthy process. Meditation can be as short as one minute. You might take the time to bring your energy up from the root chakra through all the chakras so that your energy is light and vibrating at the speed of divine energy. Even in the mundane choices, you will find the perfect restaurant, clothes, job, housing, car, parking place, or whatever you need at the moment.

Radiate out your energy from your heart chakra so that you are unconditionally loving yourself and everyone around you. Create, don't compete. Know that your energy is the connection between you and what you desire. God's energy is limitless, boundless, inexhaustible. Tap in.

> *Pictures, thoughts and feelings equal manifestation. Pictures, thoughts and feelings shape your energy, which is the connection between you and your heart's desire.*

> *Know that the Kingdom of God is within you.*

> *May you have your heart's desire.*

> *May you all be manifestations of God's divine energy in action.*

Book Resource List

If you want to grow more, here is a list of recommended books that I have found helpful:

[Author,
Book Title,
Publisher]

Dr. Joseph Murphy
*The Power of Your
   Sub-Conscious Mind*
Prentice-Hall, 1963

Ernest Holmes
The Science of Mind Text Book
Jeremy P. Tarcher/
   Putnam, 1938

Louise L. Hay
Heal Your Body
Hay House, Inc., 1982

Howard Vernon
The Mystic Path to Cosmic Power
Parker Publishing
   Company, Inc., 1967

Vera Stanley Alder
The Finding of the Third Eye
Samuel Weiser, 1938

John Randolph Price
The Super Being
Arnan Publishing, 1981

The Three Initiates
The Kybalion Hermetic Philosophy
The Yogi Publication Society,
   Masonic Temple, 1912

Catherine Ponder
The Dynamic Laws of Prosperity
De Vorss & Company, 1962

U.S. Anderson
Three Magic Words
Wilshire Book Company, 1961

Dr. Venice J. Bloodworth
Key To Yourself
De Vorss & Company, 1952

H. Emily Cady
Lessons In Truth
Unity Village, MO, 1903

Order Form

JOYCE RENNOLDS
Motivator of One or a Thousand

JR Publishing, P.O. Box 76794
Atlanta, Georgia 30358, USA
Phone 770 642 0161
Fax 770 643 1657
Online www.joycerennolds.com
E-mail sales@joycerennolds.com

name

address

city/state/zip

phone [H]   [W]

fax   e-mail address

☐ I'm interested in hosting a **JOYCE RENNOLDS SEMINAR**

Quan	Stock #	Item Description	Price	Total
		JR-2002 ***Stepping Into the 21ˢᵗ Century***—*6 audio cassette tape album* on universal laws and the changes taking place in the world today.	$60.⁰⁰	
		JR-2001 ***2001 Millennium Series***—*6 audio cassette tape album* creating more money, career changes, abundance and spiritual growth in your life.	$60.⁰⁰	
		JR-1994 ***Prosperity Now***—*6 audio cassette tape album* covers principles for success, including mind mapping and affirmations.	$60.⁰⁰	
		EC-1985 **The ENERGY CONNECTION**™—*This is the revised edition of Joyce Rennolds' popular book.* Experience the energy. Learn to turn on your mind, to turn on your life.	$19.⁹⁵	

Shipping & handling continental USA
Additional for international orders

Up to $29.99......................add $5.50

$30 to $49.99......................add $7.50

$50 to $99.99......................add $9.50

Over $100..........................add $11.50

Add total of items _____

Add shipping & handling _____

Georgia residents
add 7% sales tax _____

TOTAL ENCLOSED
[US Funds only]

☐ Personal Check: make payable to *JR Publishing.*

☐ Master Card   ☐ VISA   ☐ American Express   ☐ Discover

card number   expiration date

cardholder's signature

print name